BURNT OUT

GARY MITCHELL

T0352879

Burnt Out was first performed
at Lyric Theatre, Belfast, on 7 October 2023

Cheryl	Kerri Quinn
Michael	Terence Keeley
Donny	Caolán Byrne
PC McGoldrick	Caroline Curran
Lesley	Shannen McNeice
Director	Jimmy Fay
Assistant Director	Ross Fitzpatrick
Set & Costume Designer	Conor Murphy
Lighting Designer	Mary Tumelty
Sound Designer	Garth McConaghie
Audio Visual Designer	Neil O'Driscoll
Fight Director	Ian McCracken
Executive Producer	Jimmy Fay
Senior Producer	Morag Keating
Casting Director	Clare Gault
Production Co-ordinator	Kerry Fitzsimmons
Head of Production	Adrian Mullan
Production Manager	Siobhán Barbour
Assistant Production Manager	Fergal Lonergan
Senior Production Technician	Ian Vennard
Company Stage Manager	Aimee Yates
Stage Managers	Stephen Dix
	Louise Graham
Deputy Stage Manager	Kerri Stokes
Costume Supervisor	Gillian Lennox
Costume Assistants	Mairead McCormack
	Ciara Leneghan-White
Breakdown Artist	Sarah Carey
Hair & Make-Up	Nuala Campbell

Technical Manager	Arthur Oliver-Brown
Technicians	Liam Hinchcliffe
	Declan Paxton
	Corentin West
Chief Lx & Programmer	Jonathan Daley
Flyman	Patrick Freeman
Set Construction	Lyric Theatre Scenic Workshop
Scenic Construction Manager	Aidan Payne
Scenic Carpenter	Finn Steadman
Scenic Construction Apprentice	Jack Mcgarrigle
Scenic Artist	Chris Hunter
Workshop Assistants	Phelan Hardy
	Conor Barbour
Photography	Carrie Davenport
Graphic Design	Adam Steele

Kerri Quinn | Cheryl

Kerri has spent the last few years working on TV shows such as *Come Home, Derry Girls, Coronation Street, Blood Origin, Three Families* and three seasons on *Hope Street*, playing the role of sergeant Marlene Petigrew.

Her theatre roles include Sally Bowles (*Cabaret*); Rita (*Educating Rita*); Valerie (*The Weir*); and Jenny Diver (*Threepenny Opera*). Kerri has been a fan of Gary Mitchell's work for many years and is delighted to be involved in this new piece of writing.

For the last eleven years, she has also performed in the Cabaret Supper Club in Belfast.

Terence Keeley | Michael

Trained at Guildhall School of Music and Drama

Theatre credits include: *Mirrorball, The Nativity – What The Donkey Saw, Philadelphia, Here I Come!* (Lyric Theatre); *Mojo Mickybo* (UK/Irish tour); *Aladdin, Titanic Boys* (GBL Theatre Company); *The Ferryman* (West End/Broadway); *Macbeth* (Shakespeare's Globe); *The Beauty Queen of Leenane* (Young Vic); *This is My Family* (Sheffield Theatres/UK Tour); *Othello, 25th Annual Putnam County Spelling Bee* (Bruiser); *Gibraltar Straight, Project Children* (Brassneck); *Under The Hawthorne Tree* (Cahoots); *Franklins Fun House* (Edinburgh Fringe).

TV credits include: *Derry Girls, Frankenstein Chronicles, Titanic Blood and Steel, Hope Street, Almost Never, Paddy Raff Show.*

Film credits include: *71, Ballywalter, Here Before, Puckoon, Rat, The Music Room.*

Caolán Byrne | Donny

Trained at Royal Academy of Dramatic Art

Film credits include: *Star Wars: Outlaws* (Disney/Lucas Films); *Dead Shot* (Sky Films); *The Wonder* (Element Pictures/Netflix); *Sapling* (NI screen); *Nowhere Special* (20th Century Fox); *A Good Woman is Hard to Find* (Superb Films); *The Foreigner* (STX Entertainment); *The Lock Inn* (Lockinn Productions); *Florence Foster Jenkins* (Qwerty Films); *The Comedian* (The Bureau); *Mr Nice* (Independent); *Round Ireland with a Fridge, Swansong* (Zanzibar

Films/Florin Films); *Titanic Town* (Company Pictures) and *This is the Sea* (Pembroke Productions).

Television credits include: *Das Boot* (Sky/Bavaria); *Bloodlands* (Hattrick/BBC); *Dr Who* (BBC); *Miss Scarlet and the Duke* (A+E); *Casualty* (BBC); *Britannia* (Sky Atlantic); *Chernobyl* (HBO); *The Miniaturist* (The Forge/BBC); *Porridge* (BBC); *Will* (Turner Network TV); *Harley and the Davidsons* (Discovery USA); *The Rack Pack* (BBC); *Vera* (ITV); *Mrs Brown's Boys* (BBC Scotland); *Wodehouse in Exile* (BBC); *Titanic Blood and Steel* (Starz) and *The Message* (BBC).

Theatre credits include: *The Beauty Queen of Leenane* (Lyric Theatre Belfast/Prime Cut); *Macbeth* (New York Theatre Workshop); *Othello* (New York Theatre Workshop); *Particle Of Dread* (Field Day Theatre Company); *The Magic* (Soho Theatre/Edinburgh Festival); *Over The Bridge* (Finborough Theatre); *Scenes from the Enquiry* (The Mac); *Love's Labours Lost* (Guildford Shakespeare Company); *The Tempest* (Guildford Shakespeare Company), *The Playboy of the Western World* (Nuffield Theatre Southampton); *The Flags* (Hull Truck Theatre); *A Tale for Winter* (Quicksilver/National Tour); *King Lear* (Royal Shakespeare Company/West End), *Romeo and Juliet* (Royal Shakespeare Company); *Macbeth* (Royal Shakespeare Company), *The Cherry Orchard* (Acting Shakespeare Company) and *Cinderella* (Couch Potato Productions).

Caroline Curran | PC McGoldrick

Caroline is an actress and writer from Belfast. She received a BA Hons in Drama from Queen's University. Her credits include: *Jingle All the Hairspray* (Theatre at the Mill); *Rough Girls* (Lyric Theatre); *2050 Under the Albert Clock* (Lyric Theatre); *Buttercup* (Spanner in the Works); *Soft Border Patrol* (BBC NI); *The Real Housewives of Norn Iron* (Grand Opera House, Belfast); *It's a Wonderful Wee Christmas* (Theatre at the Mill); *Diablo*(Lyric/ southern tour/ Canada/southern tour/Dublin tour); *Maggie Yer Ma* (GOH); *Maggie's Feg Run* (The Metropolitan Arts Centre, Belfast/ GOH/tour); *The Nightshift Before Christmas* (Theatre at the Mill); *Holy Holy Bus* (Lyric/GOH/Brassneck); *Crazy* (GBL Productions/ GOH/The MAC); *Entitled* (Macha Productions/The MAC); *Last Orders at The Rough Diamond* (Theatre at the Mill); *My Big Fat Belfast Christmas* (Theatre at the Mill); *Dirty Dancing in le Shebeen*

(The MAC/GOH); *50 Shades of Red, White and Blue* (The MAC/GOH, Belfast/tour), *The Glass Bell* (The MAC); *Notorious* (Spanner in the Works); *Eternally Scrooged* (Terra Nova); *Diablo and Well Behaved Women Rarely Make History* (Lyric Theatre, Belfast/Edinburgh Fringe/Brighton Fringe); *Ulster Kama Sutra* (Terra Nova Productions); *Carol's Christmas* (written by Nuala McKeever); *The Christening* (Rawlife Theatre Co); *Popping Candy* (Spanner in the Works Theatre Company); *Hostel* (Slide Away Productions/Kabosh); *ToBeboorNottoBebo*, *Life Goes On* and *Cuss the World* (Spanner in the Works Theatre Company).

She was at the Buxton Fringe with Spanner in the Works Theatre Company when they won Best Production 2021.

Shannen McNeice | Lesley

Shannen McNeice is a Belfast born actor based in Belfast. She started her training with The Lyric Drama Studio and then went on to train at The Royal Welsh College of Music and Drama. During her time at Royal Welsh, Shannen won a Laurence Olivier Bursary Award and was also nominated for an Evening Standard Future Theatre Fund Award.

She is the Replay Theatre Company Fellow of 2023–24 and is working towards creating her first inclusive piece of theatre for young audiences.

Shannen is delighted to be back playing Lesley in Burnt Out after being a part of this show in 2020 for Listen at The Lyric.

Some of her past credits include *The Shedding of Skin* (Kabosh Theatre Company); *A Walk is Not Just a Walk* (Lyric Theatre Belfast/Frantic Assembly); *Burnt Out* by Gary Mitchell for Listen at the Lyric and *Dance Nation* (The Richard Burton Company).

Gary Mitchell | Playwright

Gary Mitchell is an internationally recognised, multi-award winning, writer from Northern Ireland. In 1998 he was made Writer in Residence at the Royal National Theatre in London, and his plays have been performed at a variety of leading theatres including the Royal Court (Upstairs and Downstairs), the Abbey Theatre (Dublin) and the Lyric Theatre (Belfast). Awards include the Pearson Best New Play Award, the George Devine Award, the Evening Standard Charles Wintour Award for Most Promising New Playwright and the *Irish Times* Theatre Award for Best New Play. Critics have raved about his work and the *Guardian* has declared him to be 'one of the most talked about voices in European Theatre' and 'arguably Northern Ireland's greatest playwright'.

Jimmy Fay | Director

Jimmy Fay is the Executive Producer and Artistic Director of the Lyric Theatre, Belfast.

Jimmy is a former acting Literary Director of the Abbey Theatre where he was also an Associate Director and Staff Director.

He formed his own company, Bedrock Productions, in 1993 which he ran until 2010. He co-founded the Dublin Fringe Festival in 1995 and was its first director in 1995 and 1996.

His directing credits include: *Blasted* by Sarah Kane, *Faraway* by Caryl Churchill, *East* by Stephen Berkoff, *Night Just Before the Forest*, *Quay West* and *Roberto Zucco* by Bernard Marie Koltes, *wideboy gospel* by Ken Harmon, *Quartet* by Heiner Muller, *Deep Space* by Alex Johnston, *This is Our Youth* by Kenneth Lonergan and he curated Electroshock, a Theatre of Cruelty Season all for Bedrock at the Project Arts Centre.

For the Lyric: *Pentecost* by Stewart Parker, *Double Cross* by Tom Kilroy, *Here Comes the Night* by Rosemary Jenkinson and *St Joan* by George Bernard Shaw, *True West* by Sam Shepard.

For Tinderbox: *The Chairs* by Ionesco adapted by Owen McCafferty, and was part of the directing team on *Convictions* at the Crumlin Road Court.

For Abbey Theatre: *A School for Scandal* by RB Sheridan, *The Resistible Rise of Artuo Ui* by Brecht, *Saved* by Edward Bond, *True West, Curse of the Starving Class* and *Ages of the Moon* by Sam Shepard, *Playboy* by Bisi Adigun and Roddy Doyle, *A Government Inspector* by Gogol adapted by Roddy Doyle, *Macbeth* and *Henry IV* by Shakespeare, *Melonfarmer* by Alex Johnston, *At Swim Two Birds* by Flann O'Brian. and *The Risen People* by James Plunkett

Dream Play by Strinberg/Churchill for the National Youth Theatre

The Gods Are Not to Blame by Ola Rotimi (co-directed with Bisi Adigun) for Arambe Productions.

For Landmark Productions – *The Last Days of the Celtic Tiger, Between Foxrock and a Hard Place, Breaking Dad and Postcards from the Ledge* by Paul Howard

For Bickerstaff Comedians by Trevor Griffith, *Rap Eire* by Des Bishop and Arthur Riordan.

He won the Irish Times Directors Award in 2007.

The Lyric won the The Stage's Theatre of the Year, 2023.

Jimmy serves on the board of the Tyrone Guthrie Centre, a retreat for artists in Annaghmakerrig, Co. Monaghan.

Ross Fitzpatrick | Assistant Director

Ross Fitzpatrick is an Irish actor/writer/director. He trained in Drama (Performance) in Dublin's Conservatoire of Music and Drama and is currently under the directorial mentorship of Emma Jordan.

Most recently he was the Assistant Director of the critically acclaimed *The Beauty Queen of Leenane* alongside Emma Jordan in the Lyric Theatre, Belfast. Ross also originated the part of Mick Landry (and twelve other characters) in the professional premiere of Colin Murphy's site-specific documentary play *The Asylum Workshop*. Other stage credits include: Romeo in *Romeo and Juliet* at the dlr Mill Theatre, Swing in *Julius Caesar* (dir. Aoife Spillane-Hinks), Witch/Fleance/Captain/Young Siward in *Macbeth,* Tybalt in *Romeo and Juliet* and understudy for *Little Red* at the dlr Mill Theatre, Romeo in *Romeo and Juliet* (dir. Miriam O'Meara), Witch/ Johannes/ Prince in *Grimm Tales* (Smock Alley Main Stage), Bill in *The Panel* (Peacock stage – Abbey Theatre), James in *Chromatics* (dir. Andrew Keates), Arlecchino in *Commedia Marketplace* and Beast in *Beauty and The Beast*. Screen and voiceover credits include the award-winning Irish language short film *Faitíos* directed by Martha Fitzgerald and Narrator/Ferdia in *An Táin* directed by Miriam O'Meara. Ross was also a playwright in residence in the Axis Theatre as part of the *Axis Assemble* programme.

Conor Murphy | Set & Costume Designer

Conor was born in Omagh, studied theatre design in London and gained an MA in scenography in Holland.

Recent designs at the Lyric include *Propaganda* and *Agreement*. His designs for theatre include *The Government Inspector, The Resistible Rise of Arturo Ui, Woman and Scarecrow* and *The Crucible* (Abbey Theatre, Dublin); *The Birthday Party* and *Juno and the Paycock*

(Bristol Old Vic) and *Richard III* (West Yorkshire Playhouse). Opera designs include *Prince Hodong* (Korea); *Alceste* (Lisbon); *Tristan und Isolde* (Hannover); *Elektra* (Gothenburg); *Orphée et Eurydice* (Royal Opera and La Scala, Milan); *Lohengrin* (Royal Swedish Opera); *La clemenza di Tito* (Opera North); *La Bohème, Wake, Turn of the Screw* (Nationale Reisopera); *Salome* (Montpellier); *Powder Her Face* (Royal Opera) and *Die Zauberflöte* (Korea National Opera). Designs for dance include *Labyrinth of Love* and *Tomorrow* (Rambert), *The Four Seasons* (Birmingham Royal Ballet), *Carmen* and *Giselle Reloaded* (Donlon Dance Company).

Musicals include *West Side Story* (South African tour) and *Chicago* (Braunschweig, Germany). At World Stage Design, 2013, he was awarded 'exceptional achievement across all categories'. At World Stage Design, 2017, his designs for *Orphée et Eurydice* received the bronze award for Performance Design. He was awarded Best Set Design for *West Side Story* at the 2018 Naledi Theatre Awards in South Africa.

Mary Tumelty | Lighting Designer

Mary Tumelty, born and lives in Belfast, graduated from Queen's University, Belfast in 2004 with a BA in Drama Studies. She trained at the Grand Opera House, Belfast in Lighting, Sound and Stage Management for two years. In 2006 she moved to a full time permanent position within the Brian Friel Theatre at Queen's University as a theatre instructor.

Recent Lighting design credits include; *Abomination* by The Belfast Ensemble & Outburst Festival (Lyric Theatre), which received an Irish Times Theatre Award for Best Opera 2020. *Kindermusik* (Belfast Children's Festival); *The Saviour* by Landmark Productions (The Everyman Theatre, Cork); *Body Politics* by MACHA Productions (MAC, Belfast, Brian Friel Theatre)*; A Night in November* by Soda Bread Theatre Company (MAC, Belfast); *Pinocchio* (The Lyric Theatre); *How to Bury a Dead Mule* (Lyric Studio); *Blue Stockings* (Lyric Studio); *Abomination* (Abbey Theatre, Dublin); *Birds of Passage in the Half Light, Tinderbox* (Gilded Balloon Edinburgh); *Propaganda*, Lyric Theatre & The Belfast Ensemble (Lyric Theatre); *The Snow Queen* (Lyric Theatre); *Silent Trade* (Lyric Studio); Kabosh Theatre Company; *Agreement* (Lyric Theatre).

Relights: *The Dead An Opera* (The Gaiety Theatre, Dublin);
Backwards Up A Rainbow, Landmark Productions (Pavilion Theatre,
Dun Laoghaire).

Film credits include: *Ten Plagues* (The Belfast Ensemble);
Democracy Dances (Orchestra and Electronics collaboration);
Ulster Orchestra and The Belfast Ensemble (Waterfront Hall); *The
Musician* (Lyric Theatre); The Belfast Ensemble. *Conversations with
Friends* (Lyric Theatre); CWF Productions (Element Pictures/BBC
Three/Hulu)

Mary is delighted to be working on the production *Burnt Out*.

Garth McConaghie | Sound Designer

Garth has worked extensively as a composer, sound designer,
musical director, arranger and music producer for studios, theatre,
film and television.

Recent TV/radio credits include: *Derry Girls* (Hat Trick
Productions, Channel 4); *Flight* (BBC 1/BBC 4); *My Mother and
Other Strangers* (BBC 1); *Malaria* (BBC Comic Relief); *Days Like
This* (BBC NI, nominated for IFTA); *Wee Wise Words* (BBC NI);
Not Now Farley (BBC Learning Zone); *On The Air* (BBC NI); *Ulster
Volunteers* (RTE); *A Year in Sex City* (Doubleband Films/BBC 1).

Recent theatre credits include: *Rebus: A Game Called Malice*
(Queen's Theatre, Hornchurch); *Frankenstein's Monster is Drunk
and the Sheep Have All Jumped the Fences* (Big Telly Theatre
co.); *The Gap Year* (Lyric Theatre, Belfast); *Xntigone* (Prime Cut
Productions/MAC, Belfast); *The Border Game* (Lyric Theatre/Prime
Cut Production); *A Night in November* (Soda Bread, Chiswick
Playhouse); *Mojo Mickybo* (Bruiser); *In the Name of the Son* (GBL
productions); *A Christmas Carol* (MAC, Belfast); *Rebus: Long
Shadows* (Birmingham Repertory Theatre); *The Miami Showband
Story* (GBL productions/Grand Opera House, Belfast/ Gaiety
Theatre, Dublin); *Bouncers* (Big Telly / MAC belfast); *Spud!* (Lyric
Theatre, Belfast); *Freak Show* (Big Telly); *Tamed* (Southwark
Playhouse, London); *The Elves and the Shoemaker* (MAC Belfast,
Cahoots NI).

Neil O'Driscoll | Audio Visual Designer

Neil O'Driscoll is a multidisciplinary artist who produces work for stage and screen and maintains a practice as illustrator and painter. He completed a degree in Film and TV in 2008 (Edinburgh College of Art), following qualifications in animation and crafts from Ballyfermot Senior College and Grennan Mill Craft School, Kilkenny. Neil has written and directed several short films and a web series, as well as illustrating comic books and moving into video design in 2012 with Owen McCafferty's *Quietly* (Peacock, dir: Jimmy Fay). He has also designed video for numerous stage works, most recently working on *Fun Home* at the Gate Theatre, Dublin (Dir. Roisín McBrinn).

Ian McCracken | Fight Director

Ian is stage combat tutor and fight director with a career spanning over twenty years. He has been resident instructor at The Oxford School of Drama since 2004 and has worked at drama schools including GSA, Arts Ed, The Royal Academy of Music and the Lyric Belfast for the Creative Learning Department.

Ian's fight directing credits include: *What's in a Name* (Birmingham Rep) *Robin Hood, Sinbad* (Theatre Royal Stratford East); *Romeo & Juliet, Twelfth Night, The Rover, Plasticine* (The Southwark playhouse); *Days of Significance, Blue Stockings, Welcome to Theobes* (Royal and Derngate); *Sweeney Todd* (RAM); *Romeo and Juliet* (Watermill Theatre); *All Day Permanent Red* (Royal Court); *Blue Stockings, Peter Pan, Playboy of the Western World, A Streetcar Named Desire, Dracula, Eternal Love, Blackout, How Many Miles to Babylon* (The Lyric Belfast).

His Film/TV credits include *Hollyoaks, Intergallectic Combat, Snake Pit, The Job* and *Fly Trap*.

He has also been Fight Captain for the Royal Opera House, Covent Garden, training some of the world's leading opera singers, as well as performing beside them in *Romeo and Julliet* and *Simon Boccanegra*.

LYRIC

The Lyric Theatre is a playhouse for all.

We are a shared, open, welcoming place to meet and exchange ideas; changing lives through our commitment to creativity and cultural talent.

Since 1951, this special place has been a springboard for internationally acclaimed playwrights, poets, directors and actors, helping to showcase talent across the world – including touring our production of *Good Vibrations* to the Irish Arts Center New York.

As Northern Ireland's only full-time theatre to produce its own productions from page to stage, we care deeply about maintaining a high-quality and inclusive programme that captures the imaginations of our audiences. We were named *The Stage*'s UK Theatre of the Year 2023 in recognition of the massive impact we make off our stages, doing things most of us don't ever see – supporting hundreds of writers to develop their work; directly engaging with tens of thousands of children and young people every year in communities and schools; creating pathways to employment; and nurturing and training young actors through our Drama Studio.

OUR MISSION

We are a shared civic space for artists and audiences alike; a creative hub for theatre-making, nurturing talent and promoting the critical role of the arts in society. Our mission is to create, entertain, and inspire.

OUR VALUES

We are welcoming: The Lyric Theatre is an inclusive and accessible space for all: a creative place to play, learn, question and explore.

We are nurturing: Our goal is to galvanise, and empower artists, whilst nurturing new generations of talent through the Lyric Drama Studio and our Creative Learning and New Writing programmes.

We inspire and entertain: We aim to provide theatre experiences that entertain and inspire; challenging audiences to explore their own and other stories.

www.lyrictheatre.co.uk

BURNT OUT

Gary Mitchell

To Alison

For the best of times
Stephen, Rachel, Harry, Lewis, and David
Sandra and Chuck Mitchell

For helping me survive the worst of times
Eileen Gunn, Justine Palmer, the Royal Literary Fund.
Sarah Baxter, Society of Authors. Nick Kent, and Nigel Levy.

Special thanks to Jimmy Fay, Rebecca Mairs, and the board
and staff of Lyric Theatre, Belfast.

In memory of Pam Brighton.

Characters

CHERYL
MICHAEL, *Cheryl's husband*
DONNY, *Michael's brother*
PC MCGOLDRICK
LESLEY

The play takes place in the living room.

Scene One

MICHAEL *and* CHERYL *finish their candlelit dinner.*
CHERYL *begins to clear the table.*

MICHAEL. You can't stand the mess for one night, can you?

CHERYL. I'm doing you a favour, buddy, don't question my motives. Am I giving this to Lancer or are we thinking of heating it up later on?

MICHAEL. Don't wake the dog. I'll clear the table while you search for a movie.

CHERYL. As soon as you open the door the cat will walk in.

MICHAEL. That's hardly likely. I haven't seen her today at all.

CHERYL. I saw her when I fed her at lunchtime.

MICHAEL. No you didn't because the ham I cut up for her was still on the top of her dish.

CHERYL. You said you weren't going to give her ham any more.

MICHAEL *takes the dishes away.* CHERYL *moves the table to the side of the room.* MICHAEL *returns.* CHERYL *dances.*

Do you want to dance?

MICHAEL. Have you forgotten how many times I stood on your feet at our wedding?

CHERYL. Maybe we should watch the wedding DVD and jog my memory.

MICHAEL. I don't want to put the TV on any more. I want to talk about something.

CHERYL. I knew there was a reason for you making the dinner. Let's hear it.

MICHAEL. Don't be saying it like I had a plan, I just wanted to make the dinner so we could have a nice night. I suggested watching a movie.

CHERYL. And now you've changed your mind because you want to talk about something. This might work on the children you teach but it doesn't work on me.

MICHAEL. Cheryl? First of all, I can't slide anything by the children; they're getting smarter every year. And secondly, this really has just come to my mind.

CHERYL. Is it about the animals? Promise me, we're not going to argue about letting Lancer sleep inside the house. He's a guard dog, not a house dog. I don't want him getting soft and I'm not going to let you use him as an excuse to let the cat sleep on our bed.

MICHAEL. I'm well aware you think I should be throwing Scamper out at night. Lancer's your dog, so he sleeps where you say he sleeps.

CHERYL. Stop stalling. Just ask me so we can get it over with.

MICHAEL. A conversation isn't something you get over with; a conversation is something to be enjoyed.

CHERYL. Are you enjoying this one?

MICHAEL. How happy would you say you were right now?

CHERYL. Do you mean right now this second?

MICHAEL. No, I mean, in life, day to day, living with me and the two pets, in this house, going to work, all that, how happy would you say you were? On a scale of one to ten, one being completely miserable, contemplating suicide and ten being you just won the EuroMillions.

CHERYL. Give me an example of a five.

MICHAEL. I can't think of a five. Why, do you feel like a five?

CHERYL. If I say nine will you put a movie on?

MICHAEL. I only want you to say nine if you mean nine.

CHERYL. Okay. Nine.

MICHAEL. Me too. Now, what would make it a ten?

CHERYL. You just said, winning the EuroMillions.

MICHAEL. What else though? Can you think of something that would make us feel like ten without winning anything or without involving luck, just something that we could decide to do that would make us so happy we would say ten?

CHERYL. I don't know what would make us a ten. But you do, right?

MICHAEL. I have an idea. That's all. We've been together for a long time now and I think we've done really well with the dog and the cat. We take good care of them.

CHERYL. We're not getting another animal, Michael. No way. We've stopped going out because of the two animals we already have.

MICHAEL. I want to have a baby.

CHERYL. I want you to have a baby too, but science just hasn't developed enough.

MICHAEL. I lied. I'm ten. I'm the luckiest, happiest person in the world and I want to spread that happiness. We have enough money, we have the house, we have two cars, two pets and we have each other. Sometimes I think nothing could happen in the whole wide world to damage what we have...

CHERYL. Don't say that. Don't ever say 'nothing could damage what we have' because that's just like opening a door to every evil under the sun.

MICHAEL. We're not superstitious.

CHERYL. Let's take a step back and think about how we ended up being so happy. You had your life as a competent, primary-school teacher and I had my life as a hot, sexy hairdresser and then we came together. We pooled our resources and made ourselves happier. I own my own salon

now and you're chasing the vice principal job and you're
going to get it one day, I know it. Now, when you lived in
your house and I lived in my house we were both paying
mortgages. Now, we only pay half a mortgage each. We also
pay half the electric and gas bills each.

MICHAEL. Which means we can afford a baby now.

CHERYL. Let me finish. You have a cat and I have a dog. And
we both agreed that when they die, we won't be getting any
more animals.

MICHAEL. Because we will have children.

CHERYL. No, because that will end the vet bills, the pet food
bills, the cleaning up.

MICHAEL. Not everything is about money.

CHERYL. I know it isn't. It's about compromise. I love my dog
and you love your cat. I have practical reasons for having a
dog and you have your silly reasons for having a cat. But I
am prepared to forgo the benefits of a dog because it would
be wrong for me to ask you to give up your cat while I keep
my dog.

MICHAEL. I don't want this to turn into an argument about cats
and dogs.

CHERYL. It's not an argument, Michael love. Nobody breaks
into a house with a huge German Shepherd in the garden. He
also helps us keep in shape with all the walking. You like my
shape and I like your shape. You can't take a cat for a walk
and if somebody broke in, your cat would probably help
them find our valuables.

MICHAEL. You don't have to pick cat shit up from the garden
or carry a pooper scooper everywhere and here we go, you're
sucking me into this.

CHERYL. I'm not. What I'm saying is we're right to cut back
on how many mouths we have to feed. I don't need a guard
dog when I have you. And you don't need a cat to give you
affection when you have me.

MICHAEL. The cat doesn't give me affection. Why am I doing this?

CHERYL. My, our, dream, is to have this beautiful house to ourselves, Michael. Imagine just me and you, no cat, no dog. Or, when you get to be Principal and I open up two or three more salons we could get an even better house, a dream house. A kid, or a couple of kids, would destroy that house.

MICHAEL. Then why would we be doing all that?

CHERYL. To be the happiest people in the world. I'm talking elevens here, Michael. Pick any of your brothers' houses or any of my sisters' houses. Think about their lives. Think about their houses and the way they live. Chewing gum in the carpet. Jam on door handles. Cheeky children backtalking all day long or walking muck all through the house. Broken locks on the toilet door. Broken dishwashers, broken washing machines, broken microwaves, everybody sitting around texting all day and swearing at each other, or in your family, slapping each other or throwing weapons. Dirty nappies sitting on the kitchen table where they eat. Where they eat, Michael.

MICHAEL. They're animals. They're not doing it right. We would…

The door bangs loudly.

CHERYL. This can only be bad.

MICHAEL. Why, is it going to be evil waiting to pounce?

MICHAEL *goes out of the room and answers the front door.* CHERYL *waits and soon* MICHAEL *returns with his brother* DONNY *who has been drinking.*

DONNY. I'm not interrupting anything special, am I? It's not your anniversary, is it?

CHERYL. No. Your brother made dinner though.

MICHAEL. Don't say it like I never make dinner. I make it as much as you do. As often. (*To* DONNY.) Here, Donny, did you see our Scamper on your way in?

DONNY. No. I need to talk to you. Two minutes tops.

MICHAEL. I was about to go out and find Scamper. Do you want to go with me?

CHERYL (*to* MICHAEL). Seriously?

MICHAEL. I can walk the dog at the same time. I'll even take the pooper scooper with me. You can stay here and have a nice rest.

DONNY. It's freezing outside, our kid. I was counting on you giving me a wee lift home actually, after I tell you what I'm going to do for you.

MICHAEL. I'll give you a lift now sure and you can tell me on the way.

DONNY *slaps* MICHAEL *playfully on the head.*

DONNY. No, wee man, stop trying to get rid of me. I want to tell her too.

MICHAEL. Is it about the job?

DONNY. What job?

MICHAEL. Me and my mum were talking about Donny's work situation.

CHERYL. I didn't know he had a work situation.

MICHAEL. My mum was telling me about government workshops for long-term unemployed people and we talked about the sort of thing Donny could do that we could then help him with. For example, if he did a course on painting and decorating, we could then let him decorate our living room or one of the other rooms in the house, and then he could use it as a showroom. We could show all our neighbours and get him more work, and if things went well, he could have his own wee business.

CHERYL. Have you ever done painting and decorating, Donny?

DONNY. No. And I'm not about to start.

MICHAEL. Gardening then. People are always coming to our door and asking if they can cut our grass or clip the trees for us. There's plenty of money to be made at that.

CHERYL. They have their own gear though, Michael.

DONNY. Wise up, our kid. I'm not a fucking gardener. Now listen carefully. My ma wants me to help you with that lot over there.

CHERYL. Who over where?

DONNY. You don't even know yet, do you? You jumped out of the fire and landed straight in the frying pan. But don't worry, old Donny is here to help. But I'm going to need you to be completely honest with me, at all times. Did you complain to the police?

MICHAEL. About what?

DONNY. Cheryl? Did you complain to the police behind my wee brother's back?

CHERYL. I haven't the faintest idea what you are talking about, Donny.

DONNY. Was it that lot over there, rapping your door and asking for wood that started it?

CHERYL. Who would be asking for wood at our door?

DONNY. I don't know. Maybe the people who are building a fucking giant bonfire in the field facing your house.

CHERYL. That's impossible.

MICHAEL *looks through the blinds and then goes to the door.* CHERYL *hovers.*

DONNY. You look amazing, Cheryl. I don't know why he lets you go to bed and sits up playing his wee Playstation. I know what I'd rather play with.

MICHAEL. Cheryl!

CHERYL. No way.

MICHAEL. Scamper. Scamper!

> CHERYL *leaves.* DONNY *watches her luridly before wandering around the living room, casing the joint. He spots a watch on the mantelpiece and pockets it. They return.*

DONNY. That's just the beginning. They're only working on that wee hut. You know the one they get up to all the mischief inside every night until the eleventh? There's no Playstations in there, know what I mean, Cheryl?

CHERYL. I know all about bonfires. I'm from the Shore Road not Devon.

DONNY. They have bonfires in Devon too, Cheryl. Though that really does annoy me about the English. How they do wee TV programmes about our bonfires in a very negative way, making us out to be fucking idiots, but the exact same people don't seem to say anything when it's Guy Fawkes' night.

MICHAEL. I have to find Scamper.

CHERYL. Really, Michael. Wee hoods are building a bonfire directly opposite our house and you're worried about the bloody cat.

DONNY. Wait till you see how big it gets. I love watching the way they keep climbing up around the outside to add more and more layers. According to the ones I spoke to, they're going for the record.

MICHAEL. When we viewed this house before we bought it, nobody told us there was a bonfire site across the road. I mean, you would think that would be something people should tell you.

DONNY. This is why I volunteered to sort it out for you. I knew he would get on like this, Cheryl, but don't you worry, love, his big brother is on the case. I already went over to see the boys. Just to keep you right.

MICHAEL. Tell me you didn't do that.

DONNY. I did. My ma knows about it. Anyway, stop panicking. They're all community friendly these days.

CHERYL. Can you not hear that music? What is community friendly about that?

DONNY. Close the door, you've double glazing.

CHERYL. There must be somebody we can talk to about this.

DONNY. I spoke to them already.

CHERYL. I don't mean them. I mean a solicitor. A Catholic one would be good.

DONNY. Don't talk like that. It's a good job I spoke to them because it turns out that somebody has been complaining to the police about the bonfire, and they asked me to look into it for them. Just to put the feelers out sort of thing and find out which one of your neighbours has been trying to get it stopped.

MICHAEL. How exactly would you do that?

DONNY. The easiest way would be for you to ask them all, and then you tell me who it is, and I tell them over there. And that would be the end of the matter.

CHERYL. That would be lovely. 'Hello Mrs Jennings, isn't it a lovely day? Here, have you been complaining to the police about the bonfire site?'

DONNY. You don't have to do it like that like. But here, Michael, you do have to do it.

CHERYL. We don't have to do anything.

DONNY. Well, the faster you take the spotlight off yourselves the better for everybody.

CHERYL. Why would the spotlight be on us?

DONNY. Your house is the closest to the field, so people are going to jump to conclusions. I just thought it would be a good idea to nip it in the bud before that happens or anything else happens.

CHERYL. Anything else like what?

MICHAEL *lifts a lead for the dog hoping to steer his brother away from an argument.*

MICHAEL. Do you want to go a walk with me, Donny, before I throw you down home?

DONNY. Those young guys over there don't really have anything else in their lives to be getting on with so, know what I mean? To them, the bonfire is their lives, they look forward to it all year. They start collecting wood earlier and earlier every year and they build the bonfires higher and higher every year.

CHERYL. What's your point?

DONNY. My point is nobody is really in control of them. I mean, there are people who could have a quiet word, but I don't know if they will really listen and let's face it, they're not the brightest tools. You should know, Michael, you've probably taught most of them, or tried to. I'm not saying you're no good at your job, I'm just saying they're hard to get through to. So, if the police say somebody complained they're not going to try to look too hard to see who it was, they're just going to turn round and see your big fancy house here and think, bingo, it must be you who did it. And then, they would want to make a big example out of you. You know, to stop people from complaining in the future.

MICHAEL. Let's not talk about this. It's not us, we're not complaining and now we're telling you, so maybe you can just go back over and tell them for us.

DONNY. I can't make it up like. It has to be true, or they'll never trust me again.

MICHAEL. It is true. We didn't even know there was a bonfire over there until you told us.

DONNY. I need to hear your wife saying it.

MICHAEL. Tell him, Cheryl, so we can get this over with.

CHERYL. You know on the opposite side of that field is a children's play area?

DONNY. I didn't know that.

CHERYL. There is and it has that soft foamy stuff on the ground in case the children fall on it. That foam will probably melt when they light that bonfire. How are children going to play there after that happens?

DONNY. What's that got to do with you? You don't have a kid.

CHERYL. That doesn't mean I don't care about other people's kids.

DONNY. Is that what you complained about?

CHERYL. No but if I was going to complain that would only be one thing. The most important thing would be how irresponsible it is to build a giant bonfire across the road from a petrol station. Whose bright idea was that? Yours?

DONNY. I don't decide where bonfires are built. It's none of my business and it's none of yours either.

CHERYL. Is it not? We both get our petrol in that petrol station.

DONNY. So it was you who complained?

MICHAEL. She couldn't have complained when she didn't know about it, Donny. She's just getting on like this because you've barged in and ruined our night.

DONNY. Two minutes doesn't ruin a night. If anything, I'm trying to improve your night.

MICHAEL. If you want to improve our night, just go over and tell them it wasn't us that complained and there you are, job done. I'll even go down and tell my ma that you did a great job helping us and all.

DONNY. Okay. But I'm not going to mention the petrol station or the playground. And you two really shouldn't either. I mean it, Michael. Like not even if you're just talking to your neighbours.

CHERYL. I can talk to my neighbours about anything I want.

DONNY. Did you complain to the police, Cheryl? My brother has a right to know.

MICHAEL. Donny! Stop asking my wife, when I've already told you.

DONNY. You need to talk to your wife, Michael, son and get her in hand.

CHERYL. I'd like you to leave now.

MICHAEL. Come on, Donny, let's go.

DONNY. You throwing me out of your house, Michael? What will my ma say?

MICHAEL. I'm not throwing you out. I'm giving you a lift.

DONNY. Shove your lift up your arse. I'll fucking walk home.

CHERYL. It's a nice night for it.

DONNY. You're funny. But here, I really hope nothing happens to you or your lovely wee home, Michael, and if it does, who are you going to turn to then? Me? You're going to want me in your house if that happens, aren't you?

MICHAEL. Nothing is going to happen, Donny.

CHERYL. That's a threat, Michael.

MICHAEL. No it isn't.

DONNY. When you were a little kid in the playground and the big boys were knocking you all over the place who did you turn to then?

MICHAEL. I didn't turn to anybody. I was handling it in my own way.

DONNY. Your way didn't work well. But they left you alone after I put two of them in hospital. Didn't they? Or what about when you and your university friends got into trouble with the drug dealers who used to sell you your weed, who fucked them up for you?

MICHAEL. Again, I didn't ask you to interfere.

DONNY. I wasn't interfering, Michael. I was protecting my wee brother, like I always did and like I always will, even if you don't have the brains to ask me to. And just to prove that I'm the hero and you're not, I'll leave you with one more nugget of old Donny wisdom. If somebody comes to your door with a petition to get the bonfire stopped or moved, don't sign it, even if you want to. And here's why. They do fake petitions to get the names of all the people in the area who are against them and then once they know who their enemies are... Things start happening. You take care now.

DONNY *leaves. They wait for the door to close and then* MICHAEL *checks to make sure* DONNY *really is gone.*

MICHAEL. The bonfire being near the playground, that's a great mum talking.

CHERYL. Sometimes when I pass that playground, I stop and imagine one of them falling flat on their ugly wee faces. I get my phone ready to capture the moment.

MICHAEL. No you don't.

CHERYL. Another reason for not having a kid is Donny would be its uncle and your ma would be its granny. And I won't allow that. Dance with me.

They dance.

Blackout.

Scene Two

Doorbell rings, dog barks. CHERYL *brings* PC MCGOLDRICK *into the living room.*

CHERYL. Come in, come in. I was just getting ready for work.

PC MCGOLDRICK. PC McGoldrick. Is this an inconvenient time?

CHERYL. Well, I'm my own boss so I suppose I have as long as I need. One of the other girls is opening up the salon for me. How can I help you?

PC MCGOLDRICK. You're a hairdresser then?

CHERYL. Nothing gets by you.

PC MCGOLDRICK. I beg your pardon.

CHERYL. I just mean you're very good at your job… I should add that we are very big supporters of the R… police… of our police.

PC MCGOLDRICK. What salon is yours?

CHERYL. Cheryl's Salon. It's my name. Cheryl. Call in some time if you want me to… I don't mean there's anything wrong with your hair… I mean just call in and… We offer a special discount to you. That's not a bribe or anything.

PC MCGOLDRICK. Do you live here on your own?

CHERYL. Yes we do. I mean, me and my husband in the bathroom. I mean my husband is in the bathroom, I'm just… I've had two cups of coffee.

PC MCGOLDRICK. What does your husband do?

CHERYL. As little as possible. I'm joking. He's a schoolteacher. Primary-school teacher. I don't know why I'm talking like this. We were up so late and then this morning I was… We're up late every night ever since they… Do you want to sit down? Can I get you something? How can I help you?

PC MCGOLDRICK. It's about the bonfire site across the road from you there.

CHERYL. You know it wasn't us who complained, don't you?

PC MCGOLDRICK. We haven't established anything yet, we're just making enquiries.

MICHAEL *enters half-dressed.*

MICHAEL. Did you iron my shirt? (*Notices* PC MCGOLDRICK.) Oh hello.

PC MCGOLDRICK. You're the husband then?

MICHAEL. You're good.

CHERYL. Don't.

PC MCGOLDRICK. PC McGoldrick, I'm sorry to bother you but there's been a complaint.

MICHAEL. We know all about it, but it wasn't us. (*To* CHERYL.) Have you seen my watch anywhere?

CHERYL. The last time I saw it was on the mantelpiece. Your shirt's over there. Un-ironed.

MICHAEL. Thanks.

   MICHAEL *puts his shirt on and looks for his watch.*

PC MCGOLDRICK. You do have a dog, right? I heard it barking when I was at the door.

CHERYL. He's a guard dog, not a pet really.

MICHAEL. I have a cat. I don't know why I volunteered that information but, I do have a cat. I think it was just because she said the dog wasn't a pet.

PC MCGOLDRICK. Who walks the dog?

CHERYL. I do. It's my dog.

MICHAEL. I walk him sometimes too.

CHERYL. Rarely.

MICHAEL. I would say occasionally.

PC MCGOLDRICK. Where do you normally walk your dog?

MICHAEL. I like to walk him round the block. You know it's easier to calculate how far you've gone and all that. I'm trying to keep fit.

PC MCGOLDRICK. What about you, Cheryl?

CHERYL. I'm fit enough.

PC MCGOLDRICK. I meant, where do you walk your dog?

CHERYL. I walk him all different ways. I don't like him to get bored. I used to walk him through that field a lot because you know, before the bonfire people arrived, I could let him off the lead.

PC MCGOLDRICK. Did that upset you?

MICHAEL. If you think it was us who complained because we couldn't walk the dog through the field, you're wrong. We didn't complain, we just walked him elsewhere. Also, there were people trying to get the bonfire stopped before we even knew anything about it. We didn't even know it was going to be there, so we definitely didn't complain.

PC MCGOLDRICK. I think you're a little bit confused about why I'm here.

CHERYL. You're here about the complaint about the bonfire, aren't you?

PC MCGOLDRICK. The complaint does concern the bonfire site but it's not about the bonfire. Do you want to make a complaint about the bonfire?

CHERYL. No. Was the complaint about noise? Because we can't hear anything. Double glazing, you know.

PC MCGOLDRICK. When was the last time you walked your dog through the bonfire site?

CHERYL. It was probably up until the first night they arrived. I was too scared after that.

PC MCGOLDRICK. Do you know anybody else who might walk their dog through the bonfire site?

CHERYL. Quite a few people used to but I don't know if they still do.

PC MCGOLDRICK. Can you show me what you use to pick up after your dog please?

CHERYL. Wait. Is this a complaint about somebody not picking up dog sh– poop?

PC MCGOLDRICK. Yes, it is. Several of the children have reported incidents of people not picking up after their dogs in the field, and then they're slipping on it or standing on it and it's just not nice. They are thinking of putting up CCTV cameras.

CHERYL. Are you joking? Are you even a real policeman, person? Police person.

PC MCGOLDRICK. I can assure you both it is not a joke. I'm sure you have seen the signs going up all around here. It's a hundred-pound fine if you're caught.

MICHAEL. So, you're actually here because they have complained about us.

PC MCGOLDRICK. Are you saying it was you?

CHERYL. Definitely not. I am a very responsible dog owner. I always scoop the poop.

PC MCGOLDRICK. Can I see your back garden?

MICHAEL. Do you have a warrant?

PC MCGOLDRICK. I just want to see where you keep the dog.

CHERYL. You want to see if there's any dog shit, poo, in our garden. I'm just getting ready for work. I always check before I go, just in case.

MICHAEL. This is ridiculous. I have to go to work. I don't have time for this.

CHERYL. Me too.

PC MCGOLDRICK. I thought you were your own boss?

CHERYL. I am but he's giving me a lift.

MICHAEL. Why, what's wrong with your car?

CHERYL (*disappointed*). Nothing. I thought you said you wanted to run me round.

MICHAEL. When?

PC MCGOLDRICK. Your wife said you were a primary-school teacher, and the schools are closed for the holidays so why did you say you were getting ready for work?

MICHAEL (*lies*). I have a meeting. We do meetings in the summer. You know, to prepare for the new school year in September. It's not like we make everything up on the first day back.

PC MCGOLDRICK. Who is your meeting with?

MICHAEL. The principal. And I really don't want to be late. So, I'm going to head on, love.

CHERYL. Of course you are.

MICHAEL *goes for a kiss but doesn't get it and exits.*

PC MCGOLDRICK. My wee girl goes into P3 in September and my wee boy goes into P2. They hate school. I like to think it's because they miss their mum. You know a few years ago it was just me and them every day, all day every day but once they started school, you know. I was able to go back to work and…

CHERYL. I was going to say yes but actually I don't know; I don't have any kids.

PC MCGOLDRICK. Not married long?

CHERYL. Long enough but we just decided not to have children.

PC MCGOLDRICK. And how do you feel about your husband not wanting kids?

CHERYL. My husband is changing his mind but I'm not.

PC MCGOLDRICK. So, you're not going to allow me to have a quick look to see the dog?

CHERYL. Yes, of course you can see the dog. It's this way.

They leave.

Scene Three

MICHAEL *is sitting alone in the dark. The music is louder.* CHERYL *enters. She is wearing her nightdress and dressing gown and switches the light on.*

MICHAEL. Turn the light out.

CHERYL. Why are you dressed? And why are you sitting in here in the dark?

MICHAEL. I couldn't sleep.

CHERYL. I closed the window in the bedroom. You can't hear it any more.

MICHAEL. We shouldn't have to live like this.

CHERYL. You're right. We should live like normal people and go to bed.

MICHAEL. We're trapped in our own house.

CHERYL. We're not trapped. Did you go out looking for the bloody cat again?

MICHAEL. No, I didn't. I thought about it but then…

CHERYL. You're scaring yourself for no reason.

MICHAEL. I'm not scared and I have a reason.

CHERYL. That makes no sense.

MICHAEL. We don't know what they're sitting over there planning next.

CHERYL. They're not planning anything. Apart from which stupid wee teenager they're going to try it on with, or what stupid older person they're going to try to talk into getting them drink from the off licence.

MICHAEL. Off licences are closed.

CHERYL. I mean when they open obviously.

MICHAEL. Lancer was barking and I thought somebody was in the back garden.

CHERYL. He's not barking now. Did you go out and see him?

MICHAEL. I looked out the window. I thought I saw somebody but instead of going outside to see who it was I hid in here.

CHERYL. When was this?

MICHAEL. I don't know. I wasn't timing things.

CHERYL *exits.* MICHAEL *switches the light out and looks out the window through a gap in the curtains.* CHERYL *returns and switches the light on.*

CHERYL. There's nobody out there now and Lancer's asleep.

MICHAEL. Did you go outside?

CHERYL. I turned the outside light on so I could see everything, and nothing's been touched and the gate is locked from the inside, so unless they climbed over it...

MICHAEL. A really tall person could reach over our gate and open that lock.

CHERYL. If they were seven foot tall and had stretchy powers maybe. And then they'd have to lock it again when they left. Who would do that?

MICHAEL. Do you think this is funny?

CHERYL. You're letting them get inside your head and doing their job for them.

MICHAEL. So you agree with me. They have a job. We are their job.

CHERYL. We're not their job. They're over there pissed out of their heads or high out of their minds. They're probably having a great time not thinking about us. We've nothing to be afraid of, other than them turning that terrible music up louder.

MICHAEL. They're on drugs, drugs makes them paranoid, and that makes them think about us complaining and getting their bonfire site shut down.

CHERYL. Nobody gets a bonfire site shut down. If I thought that was even possible, I would complain and start the process, but it isn't possible.

MICHAEL. It is possible.

CHERYL. Well, look, if we lived in Bristol or somewhere that didn't have paramilitaries then I would probably agree with you, but we don't.

MICHAEL. We should complain. We should. We should make a formal complaint.

CHERYL. No, no. No we shouldn't. Because there *are* paramilitaries, and they would find out. Now you're starting to put bad thoughts into my head. I'm never going to get back to sleep and I've work tomorrow.

MICHAEL. That's why I was sitting up. So you could sleep. Switch the outside light to motion sensor.

CHERYL. No, it will keep going off if Lancer gets up and walks around.

MICHAEL. What if they've done something to him?

CHERYL. Why did you have to say that?

MICHAEL. I'm going out. (*Quickly.*) Should I go out? Do you want me to go out?

CHERYL. Do you want me to go out?

MICHAEL. Definitely not. I'm the man. You said it yourself; I'm supposed to protect you.

CHERYL. No, I didn't. We should both go out.

MICHAEL. Get a weapon. If there's someone out there, we'll need weapons.

CHERYL. If I take a weapon outside, I will use it and then where will we be?

MICHAEL. Safe.

CHERYL. No. We'll be in trouble.

MICHAEL. Let's just go and look out the window. See if Lancer is sleeping or… Moving. See if he's moving.

CHERYL. I'm going out.

CHERYL *lifts the poker. The door bangs.*

Shit! Who could that be at this time?

MICHAEL. I'll answer it, you go back to bed.

MICHAEL *goes to the front door and returns with* DONNY *and* LESLEY. *Both of them have been drinking.*

DONNY. Sorry, love, I was just going to tell Michael to turn the light out because people will want to use your toilet if they see the light on.

LESLEY. Can I use your toilet?

DONNY. Just her? If anybody else calls, I'll chase them away.

CHERYL. The toilet is at the end of the corridor.

LESLEY *leaves.*

MICHAEL. Were you over at the bonfire site?

DONNY. No. Well yes, there now but only because I was going to call up and see you two.

CHERYL. At this time?

DONNY. No. I was going to call over earlier but then I saw all them ones over there and a couple of them stopped me and asked me to go to the off licence and then I met Lesley and we got talking. I told her it wasn't you who complained by the way.

CHERYL. What's it got to do with her?

DONNY. Lesley?

CHERYL. No, Donny, some other girl.

DONNY. What other girl?

MICHAEL. She means Lesley.

DONNY *laughs and puts his arm around* CHERYL.

DONNY. Hey, you are trying to be funny with old Donny, aren't you? You know, I've always liked you. Haven't I, Michael?

MICHAEL. Yes. Let go of her.

CHERYL. Were you out our back earlier? We thought we saw somebody in our back garden.

DONNY. Wasn't me?

CHERYL. The dog was barking.

DONNY *leaves*.

MICHAEL. Why did you do that?

CHERYL. I was just asking. He might have tried the back door, he seems drunk.

MICHAEL. He always seems drunk.

CHERYL. He's out the back and Lancer isn't barking.

MICHAEL. Now he's going to play the hero.

LESLEY *returns*.

LESLEY. Your house is very fancy. That's the nicest bathroom I've ever been in. Apart from my granny's. She was rich, like you.

MICHAEL. Well, that's nice. Give your granny our best and sure we'll see you again.

LESLEY. My granny's dead, mate.

MICHAEL. I'm so sorry.

DONNY *returns*.

DONNY. There's nobody there. (*To* LESLEY.) They thought they saw somebody, but I checked and there's nobody there.

LESLEY. Why would somebody be in your back garden?

CHERYL. Lancer didn't bark. Was he okay?

DONNY. He was sleeping. I petted him and he was dead on.

MICHAEL. Why didn't he bark then?

DONNY. Dogs don't bark at me. Dogs love me. It's because I'm a dog person. Like you, Cheryl. Dogs can sense that sort of thing. They don't like our kid because they can sense he doesn't like them. They can smell the fear. Can't they, wee man?

MICHAEL. I'm not afraid of dogs, Donny.

DONNY. People are the same. Like when I walk into a room,
I can sense another doggy person. Like Cheryl. I can sense
what kind of person you are and what you're like and you
can probably sense the same about me. You like me, don't
you? You just don't want to say in case our kid gets jealous.

LESLEY *becomes jealous.*

LESLEY. Here. See if I lived in this house. I mean, I never
could, because I'm not rich like but if I did, like if I ever
married a rich man like you, Michael, I would be over there
telling them bastards to keep the fucking noise down or fuck
off.

MICHAEL. Donny, why don't you and your wee friend head on
and we'll see you tomorrow?

DONNY. What did I tell you, Lesley? Isn't my wee brother
always trying to get rid of me?

CHERYL. It's the middle of the night, Donny.

DONNY. I know, love. But it wouldn't matter what time it was,
he's always trying to get rid of me. (*To* MICHAEL.) Aren't
you, our kid? (*To* CHERYL.) See he forgets about everything
that's happened and he tries to deny how he ended up living
in a big fancy house like this.

LESLEY. Did he win the lotto or what?

DONNY. No. When I was a kid, we never had nothing and we
didn't really bother with school or nothing like that but see,
my da went to jail and all, and that's why there's a big age
gap between all of us and this wee man here.

MICHAEL. Donny, can you not head on and have this
conversation back over there? Cheryl's to get up in the
morning and go to work.

DONNY. He's at it again. (*To* MICHAEL.) Just remember
where you came from, wee man.

MICHAEL. I do remember.

LESLEY. We saw the police here earlier. What was that about?

CHERYL. You don't know?

DONNY. Hey, I'm trying to tell you something important here. Listen to me. My da gets out of prison ten years later, and him and my ma decides to go straight and to try to make their lives better, and all of a sudden, my da wants to be a better husband and a better father. Like, fuck me and the rest of us.

LESLEY. Donny, I'm trying to find out why the police were here earlier. We can do *Jackanory* later.

DONNY. Don't talk to me like that, Lesley. You need to hear this. Me and him are all right now, but I used to be jealous of him because my ma and da decided to have a new kid and when he was born they did everything for him. Silver fucking spoon, know what I mean? Everyfuckingthing, he was given.

MICHAEL. The police were here to see if we were the ones leaving dog shit at the bonfire.

LESLEY. Was that you?

CHERYL. No, it wasn't us. And when we told the police, they left. Case closed.

LESLEY. They believed you. The police?

CHERYL. Yes. They saw that we were responsible dog owners.

DONNY. I'm fucking talking here.

LESLEY. You do have a dog but.

MICHAEL. We have a cat too, but we haven't seen her in days.

LESLEY. The dog probably ate it.

MICHAEL. You need to go, Donny, and take her with you.

LESLEY. I'm sorry. I was only joking. I didn't mean to upset you. I like you.

DONNY. Lesley is a very important person. That's why I brought her here to talk to you and Cheryl. Lovely Cheryl. I dream about me and you sometimes, love.

LESLEY. I hate dogs. I don't know how people pick dog shit up. Of course some people don't. That's the problem, isn't it?

CHERYL. I'm going to bed.

DONNY. Now we're talking. (*Quickly.*) I'm only joking. Look at his face.

MICHAEL. You have to go. Don't make me wake my ma up in the middle of the night.

DONNY. Did you hear that? He thinks he's my ma's favourite and he did used to be but not no more. I am. And that's why he's now the one who is jealous of me. But listen, Michael, don't be, because I love you and I love Cheryl, and that's why I brought Lesley over to see you. She's going to love you too.

LESLEY. Donny says it wasn't you that complained about the bonfire, and I believe him.

DONNY. Lesley is the liaison officer for the committee. That's why I brought her. So, wake my ma up if you want and tell her that Donny is the hero again and her wee golden son is going to be okay because of me. Ring her now.

LESLEY. Let's go, Donny.

DONNY. I'll go after I say one thing. Just one last thing.

CHERYL. Make it quick, please.

DONNY. Oh, I would never make it quick with you, love, I would take my time.

MICHAEL. Stop it.

CHERYL. And don't call me love.

DONNY. I'm only joking. Fuck's sake. Listen, Cheryl. Listen Lesley. My ma and da decided that all the older ones would get jobs and work hard to get a little bit extra, and do you know why?

MICHAEL. You never worked a day in your life.

CHERYL. Let him finish, Michael. You can argue about the details tomorrow.

DONNY. All the older ones had to take on extra work and overtime and everything, so that we could all give my ma more money, so that she could afford to send this one to university. But fair play to him, he didn't let us down, he got his degree, and he got a brilliant job and now he lives in this lovely house with his beautiful wife and we're all fucking over the moon for him.

LESLEY. And they all lived happily ever after. End of. Let's go. And don't worry, we won't tell anybody you let us use your toilet but keep your lights out.

DONNY. You know what the irony is? Is that the right word, Cheryl? See I know words too, Michael. I know words too. The irony of the situation is now that we all paid for him to become the 'Brains of Britain', he thinks he can turn round and rub our noses in it. He thinks we're all shit. He's turned his back on his family, his community, all of us. Isn't that right? Am I lying, Cheryl?

MICHAEL. I haven't done anything like that. Sure don't I still live here?

DONNY. Yes you do, but all you do is complain.

LESLEY. Did he complain about the bonfire? I thought you said he didn't.

CHERYL. He means about other things. Michael complains about other things.

MICHAEL. I don't complain. I never complain.

DONNY. Sorry, Michael. I shouldn't have said that, son. It's just the drink. Blame them ones over there. They are the ones that made me go to the offy for them and get drink. And this one here. She is the one who got me drunk.

LESLEY. I didn't force the drink down your throat, did I?

DONNY. I think she fancies me.

LESLEY. Here. Do you want us to stay and keep an eye on the place for you?

CHERYL. No way. Definitely not.

LESLEY. Don't say it like that. We could stay in here and make sure nobody bothers you. (*To* MICHAEL.) She needs her sleep so she can go to work in the morning.

MICHAEL. We don't need anybody to stay with us.

CHERYL. But we do need to get some sleep.

LESLEY. Okay. But think about it, in case things get worse for you closer to the eleventh night. Let's go, Donny. Please.

LESLEY *practically drags* DONNY *out of the house.*

CHERYL. You need to go down and see your mum and tell her to keep your brother away from our house.

MICHAEL. Will do but did that seem like a threat at the end when she said things will get worse.

CHERYL. She didn't say things will get worse, she said, if. Now let's go to bed.

MICHAEL. He still went out the back, acting hard and trying to embarrass me again.

CHERYL. Well it didn't work. There was nobody there. Now can we just go to bed?

MICHAEL. I was just going to sit here for…

CHERYL. Get to bed!

MICHAEL *exits.* CHERYL *turns all the lights out, checks outside and then exits.*

Scene Four

MICHAEL *brings* LESLEY *into the living room.*

LESLEY. I really love your house. She keeps it well. Your wife. You are married?

MICHAEL. What gave it away?

MICHAEL *instinctively plays with his wedding ring.*

LESLEY. Your sad, dead eyes.

MICHAEL. I'll have you know I've never been happier.

LESLEY. I was joking. I saw your wedding ring. And the photos of you and your wife getting married are all over the hall as people come in.

MICHAEL. You're very good, did you ever think of joining the police?

LESLEY. I hate the police. I would happily kill every last one of them.

MICHAEL. That's a bit harsh. They're just people doing a very difficult job.

LESLEY. What is their job but?

MICHAEL. Serve and protect.

LESLEY. Serve and protect the rich. That's their real job. Try robbing a house somewhere like the Malone Road.

MICHAEL. I'm never going to do that.

LESLEY. If you do, the police will be there within ten minutes but if you rob a house in somewhere like Rathcoole, you would have it completely empty before there was any sign of them.

MICHAEL. Did you ever think that maybe you just shouldn't rob any houses anywhere?

LESLEY. Where would the fun be in doing that?

MICHAEL. Why are you here again?

LESLEY. I wanted to call and see you. I wanted to apologise for being drunk in your house last night and getting on like a real headbanger.

MICHAEL. Donny was far worse than you.

LESLEY. Was he? What was he like?

MICHAEL. Just the usual. Very drunk and slabbering.

LESLEY. Well, I wanted to apologise to you and your wife. Where is your wife today?

MICHAEL. Work. She owns her own hair salon you know.

LESLEY. She's great. You're a very lucky man.

MICHAEL. I know. She tells me every day.

LESLEY. Oh. It must be hard being a kept man like.

MICHAEL. I'm not a kept man. I work too.

LESLEY. Why are you not working today then?

MICHAEL. Schools off for summer holidays. I'm a primary-school teacher.

LESLEY. That's brilliant. I've never even had a boyfriend with a good job. I always seem to end up with losers.

MICHAEL. Like Donny?

LESLEY. Do you think Donny's a loser? I'll tell him you said that. I'm only joking. No, what happens in here stays in here.

MICHAEL. Nothing's happening.

LESLEY. I mean what we talk about. Like, why are there no baby photos on your walls? Is it because your wife's too old? That's so sad.

MICHAEL. No she's not too old, Cheryl doesn't want kids yet.

LESLEY. Yet? Clock's ticking, baby. See if I lived in a house like this, I would never leave it. I'd be in here making babies all the time. Look at my body, it is a baby-making machine. How many babies do you want, Michael? I don't mean with me. I mean how many babies will Cheryl not allow you to have?

MICHAEL. Look, Lesley, you've apologised and that's all good.

LESLEY. I've spoken to the young people over there and told them it wasn't youse who complained and I also told them youse don't walk your dog over there any more, so hopefully that will be the end of it, but for your own good, I would try to keep the police away from your door. Them lot over there hate the police even more than I do.

MICHAEL. We can't stop the police from calling at our house.

LESLEY. Yes but you don't have to ring them every day.

MICHAEL. We don't. In fact, we've never phoned the police about anything.

LESLEY. That's good because they're all useless. Seriously, the people who did complain are going to find that out the hard way, because if them ones over there find out who it was, they might just decide to make those people's lives hell.

Doorbell rings.

If that's Donny, tell him I'm not here.

MICHAEL. If it's Donny, he'll come in.

LESLEY. Don't let him.

Doorbell rings again.

MICHAEL. I have to answer it.

MICHAEL *goes to the door and returns with* PC MCGOLDRICK.

PC MCGOLDRICK. I'm not disturbing you, sir, am I?

MICHAEL. No, no. Come in. What seems to be the trouble, officer?

PC MCGOLDRICK. Is this your wife?

MICHAEL. You've met my wife.

PC MCGOLDRICK (*scribbles as she speaks*). But you're alone in the house with this woman.

LESLEY (*to* PC MCGOLDRICK). What's this about?

PC MCGOLDRICK. We're following up about an incident that occurred earlier today. I'm sorry, you are?

LESLEY. I'm the community liaison for the bonfire committee and I'm here making sure these people are happy with the way the young people are building their bonfire across the street. This is the nearest house, so if anybody has a complaint it should be these people, but they're not complaining because they find the young people's behaviour perfectly acceptable.

PC MCGOLDRICK. Okay. (*To* MICHAEL.) Is there somewhere private we could talk?

LESLEY. You don't have to talk to her at all, Michael.

PC MCGOLDRICK. In my experience only people with something to hide refuse to talk to us. Do you have something to hide?

LESLEY. That's not true. People don't want to talk to you because they don't want you twisting everything they say into something they didn't mean. (*To* MICHAEL.) Seriously, Michael. You know if you ask her to leave your house, she has to go.

MICHAEL. Just ask me what you came here to ask me and let's get this over with please.

PC MCGOLDRICK. When was the last time you saw your wife?

MICHAEL. Just before she left for work this morning.

PC MCGOLDRICK. What time was this at?

MICHAEL. Has something happened to my wife?

PC MCGOLDRICK. No, no. We just need to talk to her. Where is your dog?

MICHAEL. Out the back.

PC MCGOLDRICK. So your wife left the house without the dog? Is that your story?

MICHAEL. It's not a story. My wife went to work, the dog is out the back.

LESLEY. See, Michael.

PC MCGOLDRICK. I would have thought you would want to advise Michael to talk about this incident as it concerns your people.

LESLEY. What do you mean, 'my people'?

MICHAEL. Just let her ask the questions.

PC MCGOLDRICK. Did your wife walk the dog before she went to work this morning?

MICHAEL. Is this about dog shit again?

PC MCGOLDRICK. Did your wife walk the dog before she went to work or not?

MICHAEL. She might have. To be honest, we had a very late night and nobody got much sleep so when she left for work I was still sort of groggy.

LESLEY. Don't say any more, Michael.

MICHAEL. I don't have any more to say. She came in, dressed for work and said goodbye and that's all I can tell you.

PC MCGOLDRICK. What time does your wife work to?

MICHAEL. It depends. She's her own boss, so sometimes she lets one of the other girls lock up. That means she can come home early.

PC MCGOLDRICK. So, she's definitely in work now?

MICHAEL. Yes. You can go round and see her. Or give her a ring. I'll phone her now.

MICHAEL *uses his mobile telephone*. PC MCGOLDRICK *makes notes*. LESLEY *paces*.

It went to voicemail. I'll ring the salon.

MICHAEL *rings the salon*.

(*To phone*.) Hello, can I speak to Cheryl please? It's her husband. (*Pause*.) Do you know where she is? No? Okay. Tell her I called. Thank you. Bye.

PC MCGOLDRICK *makes notes*. MICHAEL *is frustrated*.

PC MCGOLDRICK. Was your wife upset or angry before she left the house?

MICHAEL. She was tired, so probably a wee bit upset. Why, what's happened?

PC MCGOLDRICK. A woman matching your wife's description took a dog and threatened several children in the early hours of this morning.

MICHAEL. Not my wife. My wife would never threaten a child.

LESLEY. She means them ones over there.

MICHAEL. They're not children.

PC MCGOLDRICK. They are minors. And they are very badly shaken by the incident.

MICHAEL. Are you joking me?

PC MCGOLDRICK. You said you were up late last night, may I ask why that was?

MICHAEL. We thought we heard somebody... I thought I saw somebody in the back garden.

LESLEY. We were here last night. We were trying to sort things out.

PC MCGOLDRICK. Who is we?

LESLEY. Me and Donny. His brother.

PC MCGOLDRICK. And your wife was upset about this?

MICHAEL. She was just tired. She starts work early in the morning. She needs her sleep.

PC MCGOLDRICK. Or she gets angry.

MICHAEL. No, she gets tired, not angry.

LESLEY. Get rid of her now, Michael, and me and you can sort this out.

PC MCGOLDRICK *makes more notes*.

PC MCGOLDRICK. So you were all here last night trying to sort out the trouble you are having with the children at the bonfire site. Is that correct?

MICHAEL. No, we were just clearing up a misunderstanding. We don't have any trouble with anybody at the bonfire site. Or anybody anywhere else.

LESLEY. She was very happy when we left. Because we did sort everything out and we were all very happy at the end of it.

PC MCGOLDRICK. Why are you here today then?

LESLEY. Following up on the complaints about dog shit.

PC MCGOLDRICK. But not the incident that occurred this morning?

LESLEY. This is the first I heard of it.

PC MCGOLDRICK (*scribbles*). So, you are having problems with the young children at the bonfire site and your wife left this morning very angry and upset. That's all I need.

MICHAEL. Hold on, I don't like the way you're putting that down.

PC MCGOLDRICK. Do you want to make a different statement?

LESLEY. You don't have to make any statement, Michael.

MICHAEL. We were up late because I thought I saw somebody in the garden.

PC MCGOLDRICK. And you thought it might be one of the young children from the bonfire site?

MICHAEL. Stop calling them children.

PC MCGOLDRICK. Was your wife as angry as you are now?

MICHAEL. I'm not angry. I'm just trying to explain what really happened.

LESLEY. Every time you explain something, she's going to twist it into whatever she wants. Don't you get it? They want to cause trouble between the residents and the bonfire ones.

PC MCGOLDRICK. But if your wife was just trying to explain things to the children this morning why did she feel the need to take her attack dog with her?

MICHAEL. We don't have an attack dog. It's a guard dog. I mean, it's not even a guard dog, it's just a pet. And I don't know if my wife took the dog for a walk this morning at all. What I do know is, she went to work. Why are you not writing that down?

PC MCGOLDRICK. But you phoned work and she's not there.

MICHAEL. She's trying to expand her business. She could be anywhere. Looking at new possible sites or setting up business meetings to raise more capital. You're not writing any of this down.

PC MCGOLDRICK. Here's my card. Give it to your wife when she comes home and ask her to give me a call if she wants to make a statement of her own.

PC MCGOLDRICK *leaves.* MICHAEL *checks that she is gone and returns.*

LESLEY. They want to start trouble between us. See, if they can convince them ones over there that the people in this street don't want the bonfire, then they can cause tension and when there is tension people can see things differently, and then tension turns into conflict and when that happens anything can happen, somebody threatens somebody or somebody hits somebody or somebody firebombs somebody's house or car, whatever. And if they can orchestrate that sort of thing then they can make arrests and do whatever they need to do to make it look like they're the good guys. But they're not.

MICHAEL. Well we can't let anything like that happen.

LESLEY. I agree. But, just so as you know, your wife did take the dog over this morning.

MICHAEL. You knew about this?

LESLEY. I didn't want to tell her. That's the real reason I'm here.

CHERYL *enters and* MICHAEL *almost jumps out of his skin.*

CHERYL. Is she gone?

MICHAEL. What is wrong with you?

CHERYL. I need to make sure she's gone.

MICHAEL. Where were you?

CHERYL. In the kitchen. (*To* LESLEY.) Why are you here?

LESLEY. The kids at the bonfire told me you attacked them with your dog this morning.

CHERYL. I was walking Lancer and he did his business and I picked it up and I was just coming home as normal when a crowd over there started giving me dirty looks.

LESLEY. This is what happens when things break down. You see trouble everywhere you look. Cheryl, walking her dog, obviously panicking about the complaints has looked over at the bonfire and thought she saw a lot of angry faces.

CHERYL. They were definitely angry.

LESLEY. They were more likely just hungover and feeling the pain from another late night of drinking and not sleeping.

MICHAEL. What did you do?

CHERYL. I just went over to show them the bag. I wanted them to see that I had picked up the poo from Lancer so that they would know it wasn't us. They started getting on really weird and Lancer started growling and when I tried to show them the poo, one of them knocked it out of my hand and it went on to one of the other ones and...

LESLEY. Is this really what happened?

CHERYL. They were screaming and shouting and then Lancer started barking and snapping.

MICHAEL. Snapping?

CHERYL. One of them threw themselves on the ground and started rolling around claiming that Lancer had bit him. But he hadn't.

LESLEY. How do you know?

CHERYL. Because I was holding Lancer back and he would never bite anybody anyway. Then they all started squealing and running round. One of them on the ground screaming and one of them just standing there yelling about the poo on her legs.

MICHAEL. *Her* legs? A wee girl.

CHERYL. She was a big girl. Bigger than me.

LESLEY. Her name is Stacy and she's fifteen.

CHERYL. She looked about twenty.

LESLEY. I know but if she goes to court in her school uniform and hair in pigtails she'll look about thirteen.

MICHAEL. What are you mentioning court for?

LESLEY. They might decide to take the matter further.

MICHAEL. I thought you said they hated the police.

LESLEY. They do but the hatred disappears when the possibility of a big compensation claim appears.

CHERYL. Compensation for what?

LESLEY. Fear. They seemed very shook up by the whole thing.
Dogs are very scary animals. The only thing to do now is to
negotiate a settlement. I can liaise between you and them if
you want. It is my job, like. I'll go over and talk to them and
see what way things are at the minute. Do you know what
would really help? If you made some sort of financial offer
to make it all go away and to show you didn't mean anything
bad to happen. Or maybe if you could identify the people
who did complain about the bonfire, that could distract them.

CHERYL. This is crazy. We're not going to give money to the
people who are torturing us in our own home.

LESLEY. Nobody is torturing you.

MICHAEL. If it sorts this out, Cheryl.

LESLEY. Like I told your husband. This is what the police
do. They create trouble but unfortunately now that this has
happened neither side trusts the other, so you need to rebuild
that trust. Offering money would help because it would show
for definite that you were on their side. I mean, people who
pay money are not the people who would complain or make
things worse because that would only end up costing them
more money. That's the way they would see it. How much do
you want to offer them?

MICHAEL. I don't know. I've never been in a situation like this
before.

CHERYL. We give them nothing.

MICHAEL. I'll give them something. You don't have to.

LESLEY. I have been in situations like this before. Believe it
or not, it is more common than you think. These kinds of
misunderstandings happen a lot but mainly because of the
police.

MICHAEL. Just tell me a price. How much does it usually cost
to make it all go away?

LESLEY. The main wee girl would probably settle for a
hundred quid. The one that got shit on her clothes might want

a couple of hundred for new clothes and then a few hundred for the others to keep their mouths shut. But I don't know how much to offer the one that the dog bit.

CHERYL. The dog didn't bite anybody.

MICHAEL. What are we talking about all together here?

LESLEY. A thousand pound.

MICHAEL. A thousand pound? I thought you were going to say five hundred or less.

LESLEY. I'm going to start off by telling them you're willing to give them a couple of hundred between them and then I'll come back as if I'm negotiating for them and up the offer. That'll get them to trust me and then we'll know the real figure and I'll come back and tell you it, and I'll make you look good and you'll make me look good and everybody wins.

MICHAEL. Except me.

LESLEY. You do win. You and your wife will get to live here, happily ever after.

CHERYL. We're not paying them a single...

A crashing sound is heard from the front door and CHERYL *opens the living-room door to reveal a petrol bomb has been thrown into the hallway.*

MICHAEL. Where's the fire extinguisher?

CHERYL. Kitchen. I'll get it.

CHERYL runs into the kitchen. LESLEY *closes the living-room door.*

LESLEY. Don't phone the police now.

MICHAEL. We have to.

LESLEY. Don't!

End of Act One.

ACT TWO

Scene Five

MICHAEL *is drinking tea and eating toast while looking out the window through a gap in the curtains.* DONNY *enters.*

DONNY. The new door looks like shit. I would have done a better job. What did you do with the old one? You could have given it to them over there. They love doors.

MICHAEL. We're not giving them anything.

DONNY. Listen to me, our kid. At times like this when things go awry it is tempting to turn against your own people. This is what the Taigs want us to do.

MICHAEL. Taigs?

DONNY. A misunderstanding like this can drive a wedge. Remember Cookie Thompson? His kid was hurt during violence at an old firm game. He blamed the Rangers' fans and started actually supporting Celtic.

MICHAEL. The Rangers' fans trampled over his wee boy. He was in hospital for weeks.

DONNY. They were running away from the Taigs. But he couldn't see that. All he saw was Rangers' fans and so he blamed them. It's always been that way here. Like when they had the hunger strikes and the whole world felt sorry for them poor wee starving Fenians, but nobody told them that they were IRA terrorist scum. That's the same as this, somebody has complained about the bonfire and it was probably the Taigs –

MICHAEL (*interrupts*). Stop calling them that.

DONNY. That's how it starts. Cookie would go mad if you said Taig or Fenian in front of him. He didn't realise he was turning into one himself.

MICHAEL. We're going to have to move house.

DONNY. No you're not. First of all, you would lose a fortune. And secondly, you would start to blame the Prods for this, and then you would start blaming Prods for everything that happens after this, but in fact it has nothing to do with the Prods.

MICHAEL. Oh, are they not Prods over there?

DONNY. Them lot over there probably just think it was you that complained because they keep seeing the police at your door and jumping to conclusions. Anyway, where would you go? A catholic place?

MICHAEL. Somewhere where people don't blow your car up and set your house on fire.

DONNY. They didn't blow your car up, Michael. They firebombed it.

MICHAEL. It exploded.

DONNY. The tyres popped because of the heat. And you have fully comp, don't you? You've got house insurance too I'm sure, and you can make a wee claim against the NIO, and you'll end up with a better car, your house fixed and a few quid in your pocket.

CHERYL *bursts into the living room.*

CHERYL. Michael? Michael? (*To* DONNY.) What are you doing here, Donny?

DONNY. Checking my wee brother's okay.

MICHAEL. What's happened, love?

CHERYL. My salon. It's covered in graffiti.

DONNY. Shit. I was afraid something like this might happen.

CHERYL. It was them, wasn't it?

DONNY. Blaming people isn't going to help.

CHERYL. Are you going to try to blame somebody else? I had to close the shop, or I mean I couldn't open it.

MICHAEL. Can you not get it removed and open the shop straight away after it?

CHERYL. The girls and Eamon all went home.

DONNY. Eamon?

MICHAEL. Close it for the holidays. We've enough money to close it for a couple of weeks.

CHERYL. No, no. Once we close it all the regulars will find somewhere else to go.

DONNY. You might not have regulars if they find out about the graffiti. What did it say?

CHERYL. Taig lovers. Fenian bastards. Touts. Touts was spelt wrong.

MICHAEL. What about the new premises you were looking at? Could you open the new place sooner instead and forget about that one?

DONNY. Calm down. Michael, you can't just run away at the first sign of trouble.

CHERYL. I've poured my heart and soul into that place. Do you really think I should just walk away from it?

MICHAEL. Did you phone the police?

CHERYL. I didn't, but somebody must have because they sent that woman again.

DONNY. Why involve them? They're just going to make everything worse for you.

CHERYL. I didn't talk to her. Once I saw her, I closed it up and walked away. She was looking at me as if to say, 'I told you so'. Lots of people started gathering and they were all looking at me as if I had done something to deserve it.

MICHAEL. I could go round and try to clean it all off. I don't know how to but if you tell me, Cheryl, I'll do it.

CHERYL. They should have to do it.

MICHAEL. You know that's never going to happen. Could we paint over it? I can get us paint and I can pay somebody to do it for you if you don't want to be there.

CHERYL. And then they'll probably just paint it back again tomorrow or during the night.

MICHAEL. I could pay somebody to keep watch all night. I don't have to get up for work, so I could be here if they see somebody and phone me.

DONNY. I will go over and talk to them ones over there. I'll see if I can find out who did it and then I'll make sure that it's the end of it. All I need from you both is a guarantee that you won't go back to the police, and you won't walk your dog over there again.

CHERYL. Go then.

DONNY. Do I have your word?

CHERYL. Yes. Tell them whatever you like.

DONNY. But it has to be true.

MICHAEL. Of course it's true. Didn't Cheryl say she didn't phone the police? Just go and tell them we're not going to complain about the graffiti, we just want it to stop.

DONNY. Fair enough. And no more complaints about the bonfire either. Cheryl?

CHERYL. No complaints about anything.

DONNY *exits*. CHERYL *checks that he is gone*.

I did phone the police. I wanted the workers to feel safe. I wanted something done but then Sophie said she was going home and not coming back and then Julie asked for danger money. Danger money?

MICHAEL. We should get everything fixed and as soon as things calm down and people forget, we could sell up and get out of here.

CHERYL. I don't want to leave. I want them to leave.

MICHAEL. They're not going to leave. Think about it. We're getting a new car and you were already looking at new premises. Maybe. I'm just saying maybe. We could get ourselves a fresh start.

CHERYL. I have spent years building that client base up. I know all their first names and their children and what school they go to and where they work. I know their birthdays and they know mine and I don't want to learn all that again.

MICHAEL. You're brilliant at all that. You're a people person. You'll have a new client base in no time at all and the best thing is this will never happen again.

CHERYL. It's okay for you to say that because you learn new kids' names every year, but this is different. Once you know exactly what way a person likes their hair you can do it perfect every time, and then you have their trust… (*Stops.*) We could build a giant wall around our house. Front and back and then we could install CCTV and get big gates that open when you press a button from your car. I could become a councillor and apply for the bonfire to be refused or we could buy that field over there and then we'd own it and not allow them to build any more bonfires on it.

MICHAEL. Look, you've had a bad day. I'm sure it was horrendous but all these things you're saying aren't realistic. To get on the council, people have to vote for you.

CHERYL. You don't think people would vote for me?

MICHAEL. I don't know but if we did any of those things and the bonfire got stopped, we would just find ourselves back here having this same conversation. I say we pay them off and be done with it.

CHERYL. Do we just pay everybody who annoys us from now on? Is that the plan?

MICHAEL. Lesley said they would take a thousand pounds and leave us alone. It would be a guarantee. We would have nothing to worry about and you could open the salon tomorrow with no fear and keep it open.

CHERYL. We're not giving them a thousand pounds. We're not giving them a penny.

MICHAEL. We don't have to decide immediately. I'll go and get paint. At least let me do that. I mean, you're going to have to remove the graffiti no matter what we decide to do. Do you want me to bring something home for dinner while I'm at it?

CHERYL. I'm not hungry.

MICHAEL. I'll take you out then. I'll get somebody to paint over the graffiti while you get ready and then I'll take us out somewhere and we can try to relax and have fun.

CHERYL. I'll come with you to pick the paint.

They leave.

Scene Six

MICHAEL *sits looking outside through a gap in the curtains.* CHERYL *enters and switches the light on revealing they are both in their pyjamas.*

MICHAEL. Turn the light out.

CHERYL. Come away from the window. We can put a lamp on.

MICHAEL *moves away from the window and switches the light out.*

MICHAEL. What about a candle? I don't want that lot to start calling to use the toilet again.

CHERYL. We don't have any candles left. If we turn everything out and go to bed nobody will think we're up, so they won't try to use our toilet.

MICHAEL. I'm sorry but I think I should keep watch during the night.

CHERYL. Is this because I said I was too tired for –

MICHAEL (*interrupts*). No. It's nothing to do with that. I don't think I would have been able to do anything anyway.

CHERYL. I'm pretty sure you could if I wasn't tired.

MICHAEL. My mind's not right. Even when I was kissing you, I was thinking about them. I just can't stop worrying about what they're going to do next.

CHERYL. They probably think they've done enough. All my appointments are cancelled tomorrow. Every single one of them.

MICHAEL. How do you know that?

CHERYL. Facebook. Anne Marie was on it, saying stuff about how the salon was for everybody, you know, because we have Protestant and Catholic workers and clients. The Protestants cancelled first and then the Catholics started cancelling. Probably out of fear. There was a whole hour of posts about a United Ireland and the border and things just descended from there very quickly. People have been blocking people and reporting people to Facebook.

MICHAEL. And the police?

CHERYL. People said they were going to report people to the police. Can you believe Catholics are reporting people to the police, but Protestants aren't.

MICHAEL. What about the other premises?

CHERYL. It didn't work out. Once this all happened the people I was meeting pulled out.

MICHAEL. Then let's sell everything. The house, the salon, the cars. Think about it. I could start applying to primary schools anywhere you like.

CHERYL. No. I don't want to. I say we wait them out. The twelfth will be over and the bonfire will be gone. And by August everything will be forgotten.

MICHAEL. Until next year. We could sell up and be gone by next year. You have to realise your regulars are never going to feel safe. Everybody knows about the graffiti and I'm sure everybody knows about the car and the house being attacked.

CHERYL. Then I'll start it up in Anne Marie's house.

MICHAEL. What if they find out that you're moving your business to a Catholic area? Your Protestant clients aren't going to go there, are they?

CHERYL. It's mixed. They will go there and if they don't, then we'll use special offers and incentives for loyalty.

MICHAEL. Loyalty, that's a good one.

CHERYL. I'm tired. I have so much to do tomorrow, can we go to bed, please? I just want you to lie beside me. You'll make me feel safe.

MICHAEL. We both know that's not true.

CHERYL. It is true. Besides Lancer will bark his balls off if anybody comes near the house.

MICHAEL. Good old Lancer.

CHERYL. Come on, let's go to bed.

MICHAEL. Can I just go out and see if there's any sign of Scamper first?

CHERYL. I'll be asleep by the time you do that.

MICHAEL. That's okay.

CHERYL. Is it?

MICHAEL. Yes, one of us should definitely sleep.

CHERYL. Thanks, Michael. The bloody cat's more important than me.

CHERYL *leaves*.

MICHAEL. No she isn't.

MICHAEL *switches the light out*.

Scene Seven

DONNY *enters with* CHERYL. DONNY *is carrying tins of paint.*

DONNY. The hero returns.

CHERYL. Michael got somebody to paint the shop.

DONNY. He must have got a cowboy to do it. It'll have to be done properly. Where is he?

CHERYL. I don't know. I got up this morning and he wasn't in. He was sitting in here in the middle of the night last night with the lights out.

DONNY. He's an idiot.

CHERYL. He's afraid.

DONNY. You married the wrong brother. I've told you this before. A woman like you? A go-getter like you needs a real man. Not somebody who hires a cowboy to paint over the graffiti of his wife's salon. All he did was paint black squares, like little blank sections waiting to be filled in. I wouldn't be surprised if somebody was round there painting all new things on it, already. I told you, he's an idiot.

CHERYL. And I told you he isn't an idiot, he's just afraid.

DONNY. Look, I'll paint the doors in here and then I'll do your windows and skirting boards and then tomorrow I'll go do the shop for you. I'll do it properly. New coat of paint, any colour you want. And I'll do it so nobody can paint over it.

CHERYL. And you're going to do all this work for us for free?

DONNY. No, Cheryl. I'm going to do all this work for you.

CHERYL. For me? For free?

DONNY. What about for a kiss?

CHERYL. I'm not going to kiss you, Donny.

DONNY. What harm would it do? He doesn't need to know.

CHERYL. I knew this was a mistake.

DONNY. Who's afraid now?

CHERYL. I'm not afraid. I've let you in my house when he isn't here, I'm not afraid.

DONNY. I didn't mean it that way. I mean, you're afraid you might like it.

CHERYL. I won't. I'm not. And if you're going to keep this up, you can leave.

DONNY. Can you blame me for trying? You're a beautiful woman. Does he tell you that?

CHERYL. All the time.

DONNY. What if I could make this whole nightmare end? What if I could make everything, all your problems, go away? Would that be worth a kiss?

CHERYL. If you knew a way of helping us and you didn't do it, then that tells me all I need to know about what kind of person you really are.

MICHAEL *enters through the back door and comes straight into the living room.*

MICHAEL. What's going on?

DONNY. I'm going to paint everything for you.

MICHAEL. What's this going to cost me?

DONNY. Nothing.

CHERYL. Where were you?

MICHAEL. I went to check on the shop.

DONNY. After this I'm going to go round and fix that up too.

MICHAEL. I've already done it.

DONNY. You didn't do it, Michael. You paid somebody else to do it and they didn't do a good job.

MICHAEL. It'll do.

DONNY. I'll let Cheryl be the judge of that. It's her shop.

CHERYL. It took you four hours to check the shop?

MICHAEL. No. I went to… Something happened at the bonfire site. I was looking for Scamper.

CHERYL. The frigging cat again, Michael. Really?

MICHAEL. I saw them watching me, I didn't do anything worse than you did.

DONNY. What did you do, wee man?

MICHAEL. Don't be calling me wee man.

DONNY *playfully smacks* MICHAEL *on the back of the head.*

DONNY. Relax, kid, and tell us what you did.

MICHAEL. Don't touch me and don't tell me to relax.

DONNY. Why, what are you going to do? Tell my ma on me?

DONNY *playfully smacks* MICHAEL *on the back of the head again.* MICHAEL *moves away from him.* DONNY *acts like a boxer bobbing and weaving.*

Show me what you got, Rocky? Come on. Throw one.

DONNY *puts his chin out offering it for* MICHAEL *to try to hit.*

CHERYL. Both of you stop getting on like two wee dicks. I need to know what happened at the bonfire. Hurry up and tell me, Michael.

DONNY *stops and* MICHAEL *walks further away from him.*

MICHAEL. I just asked them if they saw Scamper and one of them said they threw her on the bonfire.

MICHAEL *hides his face and tries not to cry.*

DONNY. Are you crying?

CHERYL. The bonfire's not lit yet.

MICHAEL. The mini one that they have going every night.

DONNY. They wouldn't have done that. They're just fucking you about.

MICHAEL *walks out of the room.*

CHERYL. Where are you going?

MICHAEL. I'm not talking while he's here.

DONNY. I'm here helping.

CHERYL. You should go.

DONNY. It's not like I haven't seen him cry before.

MICHAEL *(from off stage, sobbing shouting)*. I'm not crying, asshole.

DONNY. Watch it, kid. Or I'll really smack you next time.

CHERYL. Would you please do the salon first for me, Donny?

DONNY. Okay. But just remember, Cheryl. You were told. Wrong brother.

DONNY *exits with the paint.*

MICHAEL. Cheryl, Lancer's being sick and walking funny.

CHERYL. What?

CHERYL *rushes outside.*

Scene Eight

CHERYL, *dressed in her salon outfit, talks on her mobile phone as she guides* PC MCGOLDRICK *into the living room, where she has moved a hairdressing workstation to.*

CHERYL. Yes, it's me, Mrs O'Hara, I'm working from home, so I'll text you my address and postcode. You're booked in

for five thirty, just remember to come to the back door please.
No problem. See you then. Bye.

PC MCGOLDRICK *waits for* CHERYL *to finish her call.*

PC MCGOLDRICK. Sorry to bother you. Is your husband
home?

CHERYL. He's in bed. He stays up all night because he's afraid
of something else happening. So, he keeps watch sort of
thing.

PC MCGOLDRICK. What do you mean by something else?
Has something happened?

CHERYL. You know something has happened. Those people
over there have been torturing us every night since they
started working on that frigging bonfire.

PC MCGOLDRICK. How would I know that? Have you made
complaints about them?

CHERYL. My… No.

PC MCGOLDRICK. Well, if you're being tortured, I would
recommend you report every incident so that we can keep a
record and build a case.

CHERYL. We're not allowed to complain. We're not even
allowed to have the police here.

PC MCGOLDRICK. What do you mean you're 'not allowed'?
Who do you think doesn't allow you?

CHERYL. I don't mean 'not allowed', I mean we've been
'advised' not to complain. There was a complaint, but it
wasn't us who made it. Remember?

PC MCGOLDRICK. Are you under the impression that I
have nothing to do all day but pay attention to you and
your conflicts? There are under six thousand police officers
serving nearly two million citizens in Northern Ireland.

CHERYL. What? I wasn't trying to imply you didn't have a
lot to do, but I thought as you were here recently you might
remember…

PC MCGOLDRICK. The only thing I can remember is a complaint was made against you and or your husband. Something about letting your dog off the leash and intimidating the young children who were playing at the bonfire site.

CHERYL. They poisoned my dog yesterday.

PC MCGOLDRICK. Who poisoned your dog? (*Pause*.) Did you see somebody poison your dog? (*Pause*.) Did somebody admit to poisoning your dog?

CHERYL. Forget I said anything. Why don't you just tell me why you're here this time?

PC MCGOLDRICK. I have to record the fact that you are claiming somebody is torturing you in your own home and that somebody has poisoned your dog. I wouldn't be doing my job properly if I didn't record a serious accusation.

CHERYL. Are you joking me?

PC MCGOLDRICK. Accusing people of torture isn't a joking matter I can assure you, nor is it something we can take lightly.

CHERYL. Can we just move on please? I'll see if my husband is awake.

CHERYL *leaves the room.* PC MCGOLDRICK *checks the window that looks onto the back garden to see if the dog is there.* CHERYL *returns with* MICHAEL.

MICHAEL. You're not supposed to be here. You're going to get us into more trouble.

PC MCGOLDRICK. Are you in trouble now? Would you like to make a report about being in trouble?

MICHAEL. Okay. I see what's happening. We're not in any trouble. Nobody is torturing us. The dog tried to commit suicide. Everything is fine.

PC MCGOLDRICK *notes this in her notebook.*

CHERYL. Are you writing that down?

PC MCGOLDRICK. Yes. I need to close this report before I can begin the next job.

MICHAEL. Of course you do.

PC MCGOLDRICK. I'm following up on a report of an incident that took place yesterday morning.

MICHAEL. Go on. Did they say I attacked them?

PC MCGOLDRICK. Did you attack somebody?

MICHAEL. Of course I didn't. I just asked them if they had seen my cat, Scamper. She's been missing for a long time now and they were looking at me while I was looking for her, so I thought maybe they knew what I was doing and so…

PC MCGOLDRICK. Which child did you speak to first?

MICHAEL. I didn't speak to a child. I spoke to a man bigger than me. He was about six foot tall, and he was smiling at me.

PC MCGOLDRICK. So he was non-aggressive.

MICHAEL. No, he was smiling at me in a very aggressive manner. Look, I just asked him if he had seen my cat and things got out of hand after that.

PC MCGOLDRICK. Is that when you struck the boy?

MICHAEL. First of all, there's no boy involved. This was a big man or if he was younger then he was a big lad.

PC MCGOLDRICK. What happened after you struck the lad?

MICHAEL. I didn't strike anybody. I asked him about Scamper, and he told me he threw my cat onto the mini bonfire and burnt it alive.

PC MCGOLDRICK. Did that enrage you?

MICHAEL. No. It upset me. But I'm not a rage type of person.

CHERYL. He's really not.

PC MCGOLDRICK. But yet you hit him.

MICHAEL. No. I didn't hit him. I went to put my hand up, to point my finger at him.

PC MCGOLDRICK. In an aggressive manner?

MICHAEL. No, a warning manner. Not a warning, like hard warning, a warning like I would give one of my school pupils.

PC MCGOLDRICK. Do you strike your school pupils?

MICHAEL. No, I was going to point but he moved aggressively towards me, and his face collided with my hand and my finger might have got stuck in his eye for a second.

PC MCGOLDRICK *makes a note about this.*

PC MCGOLDRICK. What happened after you stuck your finger in the child's eye?

CHERYL. He didn't say that.

MICHAEL. I pulled away quickly and tried to get out of there immediately but when I turned, I bumped into a woman.

PC MCGOLDRICK. The reports I have don't mention any women being present. There was a little girl with pigtails.

MICHAEL. She was a big girl.

PC MCGOLDRICK. And you knocked her to the ground.

MICHAEL. I bumped into her, and she fell. Then they all surrounded me and attacked me, and I had to push my way through them, and I just ran away.

PC MCGOLDRICK. You lashed out indiscriminately and then ran home?

MICHAEL. No, I ran away from here. I didn't want them to see what house I live in.

PC MCGOLDRICK. And you didn't report the incident to the police.

CHERYL. We were advised not to.

PC MCGOLDRICK. Okay. Well, that's all the information I need so I'll take this back to the station and report to the officer in charge of the case.

MICHAEL. What do you mean, case?

PC MCGOLDRICK. In the meantime, I must caution you to stay away from the young children while they are trying to enjoy the festivities.

MICHAEL. Here she goes with the children thing again.

PC MCGOLDRICK. We'll be in touch.

PC MCGOLDRICK *leaves.* MICHAEL *sits.* CHERYL *checks the doors are closed.*

CHERYL. We should see a solicitor about this. This is harassment.

MICHAEL. I want to leave. Can we leave? We can go anywhere you want.

CHERYL. We can't leave. What if Scamper's alive, and she comes home and we're not here?

MICHAEL. Scamper's dead, Lancer's been poisoned and might die soon, they've ran out of animals to kill. She's going to come back. I might get arrested for this. I wouldn't do well in prison. Look at me.

CHERYL. You're not going to prison.

MICHAEL. They might retaliate. Because they think I did stick my finger in that kid's eye. You know me, have you ever seen me hit anybody deliberately? What if they have daddies and/or big brothers?

CHERYL. Stop getting on like this, Michael. It's not an attractive way to get on.

MICHAEL. I'm talking about them ones over there being linked to much more serious people. We're not connected. We don't know 'who is who', or who has control of the bonfire, or who it is up to when it comes to protecting the bonfire.

CHERYL. It's just kids burning things.

MICHAEL. Those kids over there could be related to drug dealers who may or may not take a few moments from their busy schedules to come here and kill us.

CHERYL. Nobody has ever got killed for complaining about a bonfire.

MICHAEL. Do you know why nobody has ever been killed for complaining? Because once they get a warning, they leave, sensible people leave. If you don't leave, they kill an animal. Sensible people leave once an animal is killed. Are we not sensible? Every day in this house things get worse. Donny warned us not to have the police in our house.

CHERYL. They sent them.

MICHAEL. That doesn't matter. There's only two ways out of this. Do what they tell you to do or pay them off. I offered to pay them off, but you wouldn't let me.

CHERYL. If we pay them this time, what do they do next time they need some money? They come to us again and then what?

MICHAEL. We pay them off and while they're counting the money, we leave.

CHERYL. I can't leave. I've arranged for a couple of my regulars to come to the house.

MICHAEL. Cancel them.

CHERYL. I can't. It took me too long and too much hard work to convince them they will be safe here.

MICHAEL. They won't be.

CHERYL. They will be as long as we stay in here and don't go near them.

MICHAEL. Please, Cheryl. I've never asked you for anything in your life and if you asked me I would do it for you.

CHERYL. I am asking you. I'm asking you to stay with me.

MICHAEL. I can't. I can't sleep at night or during the day. I don't even like being near a window in case they throw something through it.

CHERYL. Listen, listen. Why don't you go and see your mum and just talk things out with her. Your mum knows all about things like this and maybe if you hear her talking about it you might feel differently.

MICHAEL. I'm not going to do that. I just want to go and be somewhere else.

CHERYL. I'm not going. I'm staying. I'm going to see this out and I'll tell you another thing, if anything else does happen, I will report it. I don't mean to that idiot; I mean I'll get a Catholic solicitor and we'll build a proper case.

MICHAEL. I'm leaving right now. Tell me what you want to do.

CHERYL. Where are you going to go? I don't mind, I just want to know in case I need to phone you or something.

MICHAEL. Is this the way you want to do this?

CHERYL. No. I want you to stay with me but you're not going to. And I'm not going to make you if you're this scared.

MICHAEL. Scared?

CHERYL. I'm not saying it in a bad way. I'm just saying if you're too scared, then you should go.

MICHAEL. I am scared, actually I'm petrified. I am petrified inside my own house. Nobody should be afraid in their own homes.

CHERYL. I'll tell you what scares me more. Michael, if I leave, I think I'll be afraid for the rest of my life.

Blackout.

Scene Nine

CHERYL *is finishing* LESLEY*'s hair with a hairdryer and some gel.* LESLEY *looks in a mirror.*

LESLEY. Wow! I'm gorgeous.

 CHERYL *shows her some products.*

CHERYL. Do you use these products?

LESLEY. No but I'll take whatever you have.

CHERYL. You should use them. I don't mean that as an insult, every person should use them.

LESLEY. I will. You're really lucky to be able to keep your wee business going in your own house after what happened to your salon, but you know that everybody can see the people sneaking in and out every day.

 CHERYL *gives her lots of products.*

CHERYL. When do you think it will be okay to go back to the salon then?

LESLEY. The fourteenth of July.

CHERYL. And there won't be any more graffiti?

LESLEY. Nobody can say that. Nobody can guarantee that. What I said was I would tell that lot over there not to do any more. But I can't guarantee nobody else will do some. Though you could help yourself.

CHERYL. How?

LESLEY. Sack Anne Marie?

CHERYL. She's one of my best workers.

LESLEY. Well what about giving her a warning? She posts a lot of things on social-media that people find offensive.

CHERYL. I have no authority over what a person does on their social media accounts.

LESLEY. Of course you do. You're the boss.

CHERYL. I'm the boss of the salon.

LESLEY. Look, you asked for my help and I'm willing to stick my neck out for you, but you have to do things to help yourself too.

CHERYL. I'll have a quiet word with her.

CHERYL *goes to the door and holds it open for* LESLEY *to leave.*

LESLEY. It doesn't have to be quiet.

CHERYL. I'll sort it out. Don't worry about it. (*Pause.*) But you know what you should worry about, Donny is a lot older than he looks. The big age gap is only sexy until it isn't, men like Donny –

LESLEY (*interrupts*). You know what I think? I think you should stop seeing Donny.

CHERYL. I beg your pardon.

LESLEY. Don't play coy. I know what's been going on.

CHERYL. He's my husband's brother and he calls here to see him all the time.

LESLEY. Donny worships you. You want me to stay away from him. And you have thrown your husband out.

CHERYL. I haven't thrown anybody out. My husband has gone away because he's scared.

LESLEY. You married the wrong brother. That's what Donny always says. A frightened little boy cannot compete with a real man like Donny.

CHERYL. I've never liked Donny. I can't stand him, truth be told.

LESLEY. What's not to like? He's strong and tough and good looking. Your husband is weak and small and –

CHERYL (*interrupts*). I'm not getting into this with you.

LESLEY. I think you hated Donny being here because of how it made you feel.

CHERYL. Repulsed. That's how he made me feel.

LESLEY. There is nothing repulsive about him.

CHERYL. You date him then.

LESLEY. I do. I am. But all he talks about is you. Even when we're doing it.

CHERYL. That's disgusting.

LESLEY. That's why I want you to stay away from him.

The door bangs loudly and LESLEY *waits while* CHERYL *opens it.* DONNY *enters and takes his coat off, revealing the watch he stole earlier.*

DONNY. Hello Cheryl.

LESLEY. Seriously?

DONNY. Fuck!

CHERYL. What do you want, Donny?

DONNY. My ma said Michael was in a terrible state, and she wanted somebody to check on you and the dog and find out where he's gone.

LESLEY. Stop pretending, we all know why you're really here.

DONNY. My ma wants me to fix everything up so that Michael can come home.

LESLEY. I'm already fixing things. So, don't try to make yourself out a hero for her.

DONNY. Has something happened to your dog, Cheryl?

CHERYL. You know fine rightly something happened. They poisoned him.

DONNY. Poisoned him? What sick bastard would do something like that?

CHERYL. Them sick bastards over there.

LESLEY. Did the vet say he was poisoned? Autopsies are expensive. I know when my last dog died the vet tried to get a hundred and forty quid to do one on him.

CHERYL. I don't need an autopsy to tell me what I already know. What everybody knows.

DONNY. That's why Michael ran away. You know that, don't you? He's scared. They burned his cat alive, poisoned your dog and if you don't move after they do that, then you're not really leaving them any options, are you?

CHERYL. Cowards kill pets.

DONNY. Cowards kill people too. Just in a cowardly way. Sit down, Cheryl. Let me get you a cup of tea and we can sort out what our next move is.

CHERYL. Our next move?

DONNY. He's my brother. This is my brother's house. You're my –

LESLEY (*interrupts*). She asked you to leave. She doesn't want your tea. Come down to my house and make me a cup.

DONNY. Shut up, Lesley.

LESLEY. Don't tell me to shut up… in front of her.

DONNY. Shut your fucking mouth and fuck off. I need to talk to Cheryl.

LESLEY. I know why you're here. And it's not to talk to her.

DONNY *grabs* LESLEY *and drags her to the door.*

DONNY. Me and you are done, girl.

LESLEY. Is that right? I'll tell her all the things you stole from here and why you wanted the money.

DONNY. Shut your mouth!

LESLEY. He told me to ask your husband for the money, but it was really for him.

LESLEY *struggles until* DONNY *forces her out the door and slams it shut. She can be heard screaming for a few seconds.*

CHERYL. Is that true, Donny? Was the money for you?

DONNY. Cheryl. Don't listen to her. She's just raging because she thinks I fancy you. And I do but I'm not going to do anything because of it. You know me, I couldn't do anything to hurt our Michael. My ma would kill me for a start.

CHERYL. Are you wearing Michael's watch? It went missing a couple of weeks ago.

DONNY. This watch? Lesley gave me this.

CHERYL. You should go with her.

DONNY. I can't stand her and if she comes back and makes stuff up about me, just don't listen.

CHERYL. I won't. But I need you to leave. And if you don't, I will get the police to make you leave.

DONNY. What good did the police do you last time? Think about it, Cheryl. Going to the police seemed like a good idea, I understand that but think about everything that has happened. Your cat, your dog and they send the same stupid woman. I don't know about you, I'm all for equality like but if I was under siege, I would want them to send some big men.

CHERYL. We never had a single problem until we opened our door and let you in.

DONNY. Are you trying to say I've something to do with this?

CHERYL. Well if you haven't anything to do with it then it is one hell of a coincidence.

DONNY. Watch what you're saying, love.

CHERYL. I've asked you a hundred times not to call me love. I've also repeatedly asked you to leave my house. And yet, here you are, still here and still calling me love.

DONNY. You are one arrogant fucking bitch. You know that?

CHERYL. I won't ask you again.

DONNY. Good. Because it won't do you any good. I'm not going anywhere until you listen to me. Our Michael's never had a problem in his life until he met you and you started filling his head full of shit. But that was alright because you moved up here and kept out of the way.

CHERYL. Michael moved up here to get away from you.

DONNY. No he didn't. From our Michael was a wee boy, my ma has always had me cleaning up his mess. In school when he was being bullied, my ma made me step in and sort them all out. And I did it because that's what big brothers do. But he grew up with this idea in his head that he was a big man because every time he shot his mouth off, I was there to step in and sort it out, no matter who he pissed off. That was until you came along.

CHERYL. You're wrong. Michael lived in a shithole surrounded by trouble until I came along and dragged him away from it.

DONNY. Shut your big mouth for two seconds.

CHERYL. Don't talk to me like that. I'm not Lesley.

DONNY. I'll talk to you whatever way I want and there's not a fucking thing you can do about it.

CHERYL. Is there not?

DONNY. No there isn't. Unless you phone the police, and they send that wee woman up to help you. Do that please and I'll show you what happens when women put their noses where they don't belong.

CHERYL. You threatening to hit a policewoman now, are you?

DONNY. Phone her and see what happens.

CHERYL searches her bag for her mobile phone. DONNY smacks the bag from her hands and pushes her into a chair beside the fireplace. She is stunned and frightened.

Let me tell you something. Women like you and that idiot are what's wrong with this fucking world. You think you can get away with saying anything you want to anybody because

the world is upside down. Michael knows this in his heart
and that's why he's not here, not that it would matter much
if he was but there's nobody here to help you, no police, no
family, nobody.

CHERYL. I don't need anybody or the police. Touch me again
and you'll regret it.

DONNY. Stop talking. It might not seem like it but I'm actually
trying to help you, Cheryl, love. Women like you think
you can change millions of years of human nature because
it offends you to be inferior to men. Weak men like our
Michael allow you to treat them like shit because they're
afraid of the PC brigade or what will happen to them if
they put you in your place. And women like you think
you can stop hundreds of years of culture just because it's
inconveniencing you. Lefty feminists like you don't even
understand that you are being manipulated by politicians
and Fenians into attacking our heritage, our culture, our
principles and everything that makes us great.

CHERYL. I didn't realise you knew so many words.

MICHAEL *enters*.

MICHAEL. Donny!

DONNY. Fuck off, wee man.

MICHAEL. Stop talking. Unless it's to say, 'here's your money
back'.

DONNY. What money?

MICHAEL. Lesley told me the whole thing was your idea to get
our money.

DONNY. She'll say anything to fuck me up because I've
dumped her.

MICHAEL. Why did you do it, Donny?

DONNY. I didn't do anything except try to help, and I'm still
trying to help you, Michael. I'm always trying to help you.
When a woman shouts her mouth off you stop listening,

brother, and smack it shut. I've already done it with that one out there, now I just need you to do it with this one in here.

MICHAEL. I'll make you a deal. If you leave now, I will let you keep the money.

CHERYL. Why did you give them money, Michael?

MICHAEL. I would give them double if I thought it would keep them out of our lives forever.

DONNY. That's the man you married, girl.

CHERYL. You shouldn't pay a penny, Michael. They're not worth it.

MICHAEL. Name your price, Donny.

DONNY. My price for what? Sorting your wife out. I'll do it for free, if you leave us alone for five minutes.

MICHAEL. Two thousand pounds to you if you go over and make them people stay away from us long enough for us to sell this house and leave. Then another two thousand for you to stay out of our lives forever.

DONNY. You can't pay your way out of this one, our kid. Give me five thousand pounds and I'll take your wife away for a dirty weekend and show her what it is –

MICHAEL *attacks* DONNY. *He is not a fighter and* DONNY *handles him with ease until he knocks him to the floor.*

CHERYL. Leave him alone.

CHERYL *moves toward* DONNY*, but he shoves her violently back into the chair.*

MICHAEL. Stay back, Cheryl.

DONNY. If you agree to go away with me, I'll leave him alone.

MICHAEL *tries to tackle* DONNY *again, but this time* DONNY *holds him on the ground and gets on top of him.* CHERYL *lifts a poker from the fireplace.*

CHERYL. Get off my husband.

DONNY *laughs loudly and in an exaggerated way.*

DONNY. What are you going to do with that?

CHERYL. I'm going to count to five and then you'll find out.

DONNY. Don't make me take it off you and stick it up your ass. You might enjoy it.

CHERYL. One.

MICHAEL. Get off me.

DONNY. You married a man who wants to pay his big brother five grand to leave him alone. That's not a real man. And you deserve a real man.

CHERYL. Two.

MICHAEL. I mean it, Donny. Get off me or you won't see a penny.

DONNY. Here's what's going to happen. I'm going to tie him up and then I'm going to fuck your brains out while he watches. And I'm still going to end up five grand better off.

CHERYL. Three.

DONNY *opens his belt while* MICHAEL *struggles helplessly underneath him.*

DONNY. And it was me who firebombed your car.

CHERYL *hits* DONNY *on the head with the poker.* DONNY *tries to get up, staggers, sits holding his head.*

That wasn't even five.

MICHAEL. Cheryl?

CHERYL. What'll I do?

MICHAEL. If he survives this, he will do stuff that will make your nightmares seem like a fucking teddy bears' picnic.

CHERYL *hits* DONNY *again.* DONNY *slumps down
and starts twitching, shaking and groaning on the floor.*
MICHAEL *starts sobbing.* CHERYL *helps* MICHAEL *up
and he stands in disbelief as* DONNY *continues to twitch and
shake.* MICHAEL *continues to cry.* CHERYL *hits* DONNY
again and again until he stops moving.

Blackout.

Bonfire celebrations occur offstage.

Scene Ten

MICHAEL *and* CHERYL *have removed the carpet and are
cleaning the room.*

CHERYL. That's clean enough. It's not like we're dealing with
CSI from TV, Michael. If they ever send anybody to see us it
will probably be that stupid woman.

MICHAEL. You don't know that. If they suspect us, they could
send their very best.

CHERYL. Why would they suspect us? He's your brother.

MICHAEL. I've never been this scared in my entire life. I keep
thinking, 'Thank God we don't have any children'. Isn't that
terrible?

CHERYL. I understand.

MICHAEL. You don't. I'm the man, I'm supposed to be the one
protecting you and protecting my house. I even brought up
the idea of us having a baby. What sort of daddy would I be?

CHERYL. You'd be a great daddy.

MICHAEL. I made everything twenty times worse.

CHERYL. And then you fixed it.

MICHAEL. By listening to you.

CHERYL. That's always a good idea.

MICHAEL. And then I ran away.

CHERYL. You removed yourself from a very difficult situation.

MICHAEL. But I left you right in it. Left the person I care about the most in the world to deal with the worst nightmare.

CHERYL. I killed your brother.

CHERYL *begins to sob*.

MICHAEL. Hey, come on. I've dreamt about killing him a thousand times.

CHERYL. Do you know what you should do, Michael? You should sell this place and get as far away from me as you can, while you still can.

MICHAEL. Don't talk like that.

The door bangs loudly.

CHERYL. Don't answer that. Wait. Do get it, like normal. (*Pause.*) Wait. What do you want to do?

MICHAEL. I'll get it. (*Pause.*) Will I? (*Pause.*) Should we sneak out the back? Do you want me to see if anybody is out the back? If we're clear.

The door bangs loudly again.

CHERYL. We're being ridiculous. Let's just answer the door like normal people.

CHERYL *goes to the door.*

PC MCGOLDRICK (*from off*). Hello.

CHERYL. Hello? Come in.

CHERYL *returns with* PC MCGOLDRICK.

PC MCGOLDRICK. Hello, my name is PC McGoldrick.

MICHAEL. Fuck.

CHERYL. Michael!

MICHAEL. Sorry. (*Composes himself.*) I'm just not used to having the police in my house.

PC MCGOLDRICK. You need to sit down.

MICHAEL *sits*.

Have you seen the news today or spoken to anybody outside this house?

MICHAEL. We're in the middle of decorating, we don't have a TV plugged in.

CHERYL. Our phones are charging in the kitchen.

PC MCGOLDRICK. I'm afraid I have some terrible news. There's been a terrible accident involving your brother. He... Could I have a glass of water?

CHERYL. I'll get it.

CHERYL *leaves*.

MICHAEL. Do you mean Donny? Where is he? Is he in the hospital?

PC MCGOLDRICK. No. I'm sorry to say... I'm sorry, I haven't had to do this before.

MICHAEL. Take your time. It can't be easy to inform the family...

PC MCGOLDRICK. What? What did you say?

MICHAEL. Cheryl?

MICHAEL *stops talking and waits*.

PC MCGOLDRICK (*pauses to study* MICHAEL). We were called to the scene of the bonfire this morning by the fire brigade. They were putting out the remains of the fire when the body was discovered. I'm afraid your brother is dead.

MICHAEL. Oh my God.

PC MCGOLDRICK. Other officers are with the rest of your family as we speak.

MICHAEL. My ma will have a heart attack. He's her favourite, her golden boy. I need to see her. Can I go?

PC MCGOLDRICK. We're treating it as an accident. There are no signs of foul play. Sorry, I'm saying what I was told to say. I mean, somebody else will be in touch with all the final details but at the moment...

CHERYL *returns and gives her a glass of water and she gulps it down.*

MICHAEL. They found a body at the bonfire, and they think it is Donny.

PC MCGOLDRICK. I didn't say we found the body at the bonfire.

MICHAEL. Yes you did.

CHERYL. Did you find it at the bonfire or not?

PC MCGOLDRICK. We did.

MICHAEL. He was high when he left us.

PC MCGOLDRICK. Was he? Was he here last night?

CHERYL. He kept calling to use the toilet but then some girl was annoying him, and he stormed off.

PC MCGOLDRICK. So, what time did he leave you two?

CHERYL. Early evening was the last time.

MICHAEL. Him and this girl. Not sure if it was his girlfriend or not but they seemed pretty friendly... And completely drunk. Both of them. I think there was another girl or maybe a man arguing with him as well.

PC MCGOLDRICK. Did it upset you, him using the toilet and then these other people bothering you?

MICHAEL. It's family. You put up with it, don't you? I know I do, for my mum.

CHERYL. He did say he was going to go to the bonfire. They all did.

PC MCGOLDRICK. You were already having trouble with the kids over there at the bonfire, weren't you? Did you make a complaint?

MICHAEL. Can I see my brother? Or what way does it work?

PC MCGOLDRICK. Was your brother involved in that at all?

MICHAEL. Look. We were having trouble. Donny was unhappy about me going to the police. Talking to you about that lot over there.

CHERYL. He offered to do your job for you.

MICHAEL. They poisoned our dog.

PC MCGOLDRICK. I'm sorry. They what?

CHERYL. We think they poisoned my dog.

MICHAEL. They burned my wee cat and poisoned her dog.

PC MCGOLDRICK. Was this all reported?

CHERYL. Donny told us not to go back near the police.

PC MCGOLDRICK. So, Donny told you he killed your cat and dog.

MICHAEL. Not him. Them.

PC MCGOLDRICK. So, what was the next level of threat then?

CHERYL. Are we not getting away from the point here?

PC MCGOLDRICK. How do you mean?

CHERYL. You're here to give us the bad news and you've done that.

PC MCGOLDRICK. But this is new information.

CHERYL. New information about what?

MICHAEL. You said it was an accident.

PC MCGOLDRICK. Where were you, sir?

MICHAEL. Where was I, when?

PC MCGOLDRICK. Where were you last night?

MICHAEL. I was staying in a hotel. Why do you want to know?

PC MCGOLDRICK. In case this wasn't an accident.

MICHAEL. Are you suggesting that I might have had
    something to do with the murder of my own brother?

PC MCGOLDRICK. Why did you say murder?

MICHAEL. Why did I say murder? I'm not saying murder, I'm
    saying are you suggesting it?

PC MCGOLDRICK. I'm just trying to get the facts. That's all.

MICHAEL. Really? You want the facts. Here's the facts. Them
    people were annoying us because they thought we were
    complaining about their bonfire, we weren't, but they didn't
    take our word for it and things got out of hand. Then you got
    involved but said you couldn't protect us, so I paid them off.
    Check Donny's girlfriend's bank. She's called Lesley, I think,
    she's the liaison bonfire person or whatever that title is. I paid
    her a couple of thousand to give to that lot over there to leave
    us alone, and they agreed, and everybody was happy and
    here we are.

PC MCGOLDRICK. I have to report all this. You shouldn't
    have paid them that.

MICHAEL. I had to. I had to prove that we weren't against
    them. And it worked, isn't that the important thing here?
    Now we're all safe. Apart from my brother.

PC MCGOLDRICK. Can anybody verify you were in this
    hotel?

MICHAEL. Why would I need to verify it?

CHERYL. I was with him.

PC MCGOLDRICK. You stayed in a hotel together?

CHERYL. All this had caused us a bit of marital trouble I would
    rather not get into, and then Donny was calling in and using
    the toilet and then he was inviting other people to do the

same and I just couldn't cope with it. Here alone with them doing drugs and drinking. They were in the garden doing drugs and I told them to go and then I panicked and so I went to the hotel and stayed with Michael. The last thing I remember about Donny was when I asked him to get out of the garden and he apologised and said he had taken all the drugs and him and his friends went to the bonfire.

PC MCGOLDRICK. Yes. That seems to be the case. Again. I am so sorry for your loss, and I hope I haven't offended anybody, but you've actually been extremely helpful and I'm sure my bosses will have it all sorted as soon as possible.

PC MCGOLDRICK leaves. CHERYL *checks she is gone.*

CHERYL. Can you really forgive me, Michael?

MICHAEL. There's nothing to forgive.

CHERYL. There is.

MICHAEL. Everything is going to be fine. You did not kill Donny. They said it was an accident.

The dog barks, CHERYL *looks out the window.*

CHERYL. What's bothering you now, Lancer?

MICHAEL. He seems a lot better today.

CHERYL. Don't we all?

CHERYL *closes the curtains.* MICHAEL *kisses and hugs* CHERYL.

LESLEY *appears outside, wearing the watch.*

Scamper, the cat, wanders in.

The End.

A Nick Hern Book

Burnt Out first published in Great Britain as a paperback original in 2023 by Nick Hern Books Limited, The Glasshouse, 49a Goldhawk Road, London W12 8QP in association with Lyric Theatre Belfast

Cover photography by Carrie Davenport

Designed and typeset by Nick Hern Books, London
Printed in Great Britain by Mimeo Ltd, Huntingdon, Cambridgeshire PE29 6XX

A CIP catalogue record for this book is available from the British Library

ISBN 978 1 83904 293 5

www.nickhernbooks.co.uk/environmental-policy

www.nickhernbooks.co.uk

facebook.com/nickhernbooks

twitter.com/nickhernbooks